Editor
Eric Migliaccio

Managing Editor
Ina Massler Levin, M.A.

Editor-in-Chief
Sharon Coan, M.S. Ed.

Illustrator
Kevin McCarthey

Cover Artist
Lesley Palmer

Art Coordinator
Kevin Barnes

Art Director
CJae Froshay

Imaging
Rosa C. See

Product Manager
Phil Garcia

Publishers
Rachelle Cracchiolo, M.S. Ed.
Mary Dupuy Smith, M.S. Ed.

Take Five Minutes
Fascinating Facts

Grades 4-6

Authors

Greg Camden, M.A.
Eric Migliaccio

Teacher Created Materials, Inc.
6421 Industry Way
Westminster, CA 92683
www.teachercreated.com
ISBN-0-7439-3792-9

©2003 Teacher Created Materials, Inc.
Made in U.S.A.

Table of Contents

Introduction

The Canada/U.S. boundary is the world's longest undefended border. This means that citizens of each country are free to pass back and forth between the two countries.

The world's biggest ant colony was discovered in 2002. This supercolony has billions of ants living in millions of nests. It stretches 3,600 miles, all the way from Italy to northwest Spain.

The preceding tidbits come from the *The World Almanac for Kids*, a unique and informative publication that is full of facts, statistics, and trivia especially tailored to the interests of children. *The World Almanac for Kids* spans the curricula—from language arts to science, from social studies to math—and is presented in a rich and vibrant format that makes learning fun for young students. *Take Five Minutes: Fascinating Facts from "The World Almanac for Kids"* pulls from this wealth of information and condenses it into five-minute lessons that are stimulating, self-contained, and simple to teach.

How to Use this Book

The first five minutes of a class are among the most critical in teaching for the role they play in setting the instructional stage and transitioning students into the lesson. *Take Five Minutes: Fascinating Facts from "The World Almanac for Kids"* is designed to assist teachers in this task through a variety of engaging activities that promote skills in each of the following areas:

- math
- science
- social studies
- language arts
- logic
- critical-thinking

Pages from *Take Five Minutes: Fascinating Facts from "The World Almanac for Kids"* can be reproduced for each student, partners, or small groups of students. Pages can also be made into transparencies for use on an overhead projector. Or, questions can be written on the board for students to ponder while the teacher reads the passages aloud.

This book is divided into sections based on the major content areas presented in the *The World Almanac for Kids*. Each section contains three to five lessons. These sections can be taught as a whole to reinforce a unit of study; or, because the lessons are self-contained, you may teach them in any order. You may even allow the students to pick the lesson of the day. You may choose to do this by . . .

- reading out five lesson titles, simply picking them randomly. Have the students vote on the title that interests them most. Democracy in action!

- having a student pick a number from 6–93 and teaching the lesson on the chosen page. You could reinforce certain math concepts by having the student choose a number that is, for instance, a prime number or a multiple of a specific number.

- making up a math problem, the solution of which will be the page number of the lesson taught on that particular day.

If you decide to allow students to choose a lesson-of-the-day, introduce a number line or chart to help the class keep track of the lessons that have been completed.

Introduction *(cont.)*

How to Use this Book *(cont.)*

The lessons in *Take Five Minutes: Fascinating Facts from "The World Almanac for Kids"* are comprised of three main components:

❶ **Reading Passages**—Every lesson in this book involves students in using the skills and strategies of the reading process to interpret and understand text. The topics explored in *Take Five Minutes: Fascinating Facts from "The World Almanac for Kids"* range from the infinite (the universe) to the infinitesimal (DNA) and everything in between.

❷ **Charts and Graphs**—Most lessons in this book contain a chart or graph of some kind, whether it be a pie chart, bar graph, table, or time line. Because charts and graphs are invaluable when comparing data, textbooks and reference books such as almanacs are replete with them; and students need to be comfortable with reading and processing these effective and efficient organizational tools. In addition, many of the lessons contain sidebars—paragraphs entitled "Did You Know?"—that offer interesting information that supplements the main text on the page. These sidebars teach students to process information from different textual formats.

❸ **Comprehension and Critical-Thinking Questions**—Each lesson ends with a section entitled "Questions to Ponder." This section contains four questions, with each question progressively more difficult. For instance, the first question usually involves simple recall of a fact presented in the text. The fourth and final question often asks the student to relate the information in the lesson to events in his or her life. In this way, critical-thinking skills are developed and/or honed. Teachers may choose to select one or more of these questions based on the skill level of his/her classroom. There are math questions included in history lessons and language arts puzzles incorporated into science sections. All of this helps to keep your students focused, motivated, and learning. (See pages 94–96 for a complete answer key.)

Additional Activities

The lessons in this book offer several opportunities for students to apply their newly-gained knowledge, while at the same time reinforcing a particular writing or math concept from your daily lessons.

• Have each student write one complete sentence about the subject just discussed. Specify whether the sentence needs to contain an adverb, a prepositional phrase, an appositive, etc.

• Have each student create a complete sentence that uses a particular vocabulary word from the lesson just discussed.

• Have each student create a math problem in which the answer is an important statistic from the lesson just discussed.

• As an extra-credit opportunity, allow students to write a lesson that might fit into *Take Five Minutes: Fascinating Facts from "The World Almanac for Kids."* Make sure the lesson includes text, a chart illustrating the text, and questions that both test comprehension of the lesson and expand the reader's thoughts about the subject being discussed.

Meeting Standards

Each lesson in *Take Five Minutes: Fascinating Facts from "The World Almanac for Kids"* meets one or more of the following standards, which are used with permission from McREL (Copyright 2000 McREL, Mid-continent Research for Education and Learning. Telephone: 303-337-0990. Website: *www.mcrel.org*).

Mathematics
- Uses a variety of strategies in the problem-solving process
- Uses basic and advanced procedures while performing the processes of computation
- Understands and applies basic and advanced properties of the concepts of geometry
- Understands and applies basic and advanced concepts of statistics and data analysis
- Understands and applies basic and advanced concepts of probability

Science
- Understands atmospheric processes and the water cycle
- Understands Earth's composition and structure
- Understands the composition and structure of the universe and Earth's place in it
- Understands the structure and function of cells and organisms
- Understands the structure and properties of matter
- Understands the sources and properties of energy
- Understands forces and motion

History
- Understands and knows how to analyze chronological relationships and patterns
- Understands the major characteristics of civilization and the development of civilizations in Mesopotamia, Egypt, and the Indus Valley
- Understands how major religions and large-scale empires arose in the Mediterranean Basin, China, and India from 500 BCE to 300 CE.
- Understands the institutions and practice of government created during the revolution and how these elements were revised between 1787 and 1815 to create the foundation of the American political system based on the U.S. Constitution and the Bill of Rights

Language Arts
- Uses reading skills and strategies to understand and interpret a variety of informational texts

The Arts
- Understands connections among the various art forms and other disciplines

Technology
- Understands the relationships among science, technology, society, and the individual

Life Skills
- Understands and applies basic principles of logic and reasoning
- Applies decision-making techniques

Geography
- Understands the characteristics and uses of maps, globes, and other geographic tools and technologies
- Understands the concepts of regions
- Understands that culture and experience influence people's perceptions of places and regions
- Understands the characteristics of ecosystems on Earth's surface
- Understands how human actions modify the physical environment
- Understands global development and environmental issues

Health
- Understands essential concepts about nutrition and health

How Long Do Animals Live?

Most animals do not live as long as human beings do. A monkey that is 14 years old is thought to be old. A person who is 14 is still considered young. The average life span of a human being in the world today is 65 to 70 years. The average life spans of some animals are shown here.

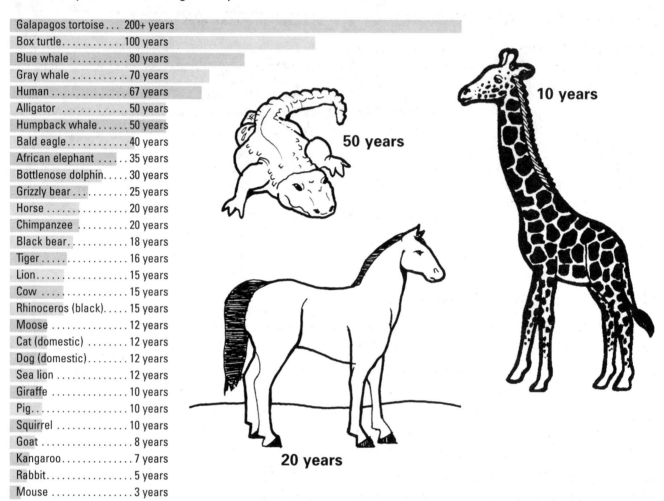

Galapagos tortoise...	200+ years
Box turtle...........	100 years
Blue whale	80 years
Gray whale	70 years
Human	67 years
Alligator	50 years
Humpback whale......	50 years
Bald eagle...........	40 years
African elephant	35 years
Bottlenose dolphin.....	30 years
Grizzly bear	25 years
Horse	20 years
Chimpanzee	20 years
Black bear..........	18 years
Tiger	16 years
Lion...............	15 years
Cow	15 years
Rhinoceros (black).....	15 years
Moose	12 years
Cat (domestic)	12 years
Dog (domestic)........	12 years
Sea lion	12 years
Giraffe	10 years
Pig.................	10 years
Squirrel	10 years
Goat	8 years
Kangaroo............	7 years
Rabbit..............	5 years
Mouse	3 years

50 years

10 years

20 years

Did You Know?

In 1900 the life expectancy of a person born in the United States was about 47 years. By the year 2000 the life expectancy had risen to about 77 years of age.

— QUESTIONS TO PONDER —

1. Which two animals live for about 50 years?

2. If you had two dogs, three cats, a chimpanzee, and a rabbit, which pet would you expect to live the longest?

3. A horse lives twice as long as a giraffe. A blue whale lives four times as long as a horse. How many times as long does a blue whale live compared to a giraffe?

4. What are some reasons why people live much longer today than they did in 1900?

Endangered Animals

When an animal species begins to die out, the animal is said to be endangered or threatened. Throughout the world today, 1,070 species of animals are endangered or threatened, according to the National Wildlife Federation.

HOW DO ANIMALS AND PLANTS BECOME ENDANGERED?

CHANGES IN CLIMATE—Animals are endangered when the climate of their habitat (where they live) changes in a major way. For example, if an area becomes very hot and dry and a river dries up, the fish and other plant and animal life in the river will die.

HABITAT DESTRUCTION—Sometimes animal habitats are destroyed when people need the land. For example, wetlands, where many types of waterfowl, fish, and insects live, might be drained for new houses or a mall. The animals that lived there would have to find a new home or else die out.

OVER-HUNTING—Bison or buffalo once ranged over the entire Great Plains of the United States, but they were hunted almost to extinction in the 19th century. Since then, they have been protected by laws, and their numbers are increasing.

SOME ENDANGERED ANIMALS

BLUE WHALE—the largest animal ever to live. Whaling almost made them extinct. There are about 5,000 in the world today.

CALIFORNIA CONDOR—North America's largest bird. There are about 60 of them now living in the wild.

CALIFORNIA RED-LEGGED FROG—believed to be the species from the Mark Twain story "The Celebrated Jumping Frog of Calaveras County." About 350 remain in the wild.

GIANT PANDA—China's most loveable animal. As few as 1,000 of these creatures remain in the mountains of southwest China.

Dinosaurs became extinct around 65 million years ago. At that time, a huge asteroid or comet might have hit Earth. This would have filled the atmosphere with dust and debris, blocking most of the sun's light and heat.

━━ QUESTIONS TO PONDER ━━

1. What does the word *habitat* mean?

2. What is the largest animal to ever live?

3. Giant pandas spend up to 14 hours a day eating bamboo. If it took a panda 12 hours to eat 78 pounds of bamboo, how many pounds would it have eaten per hour?

4. What are some steps that can be taken to help preserve different habitats where wild animals live?

Amazing Ants

Some 9,500 species of ants have been discovered and named so far. **Myrmecologists** (scientists who study ants) estimate that there are about 20,000 species in all. Ants have been around for about 100 million years, and are found in just about every type of land environment.

WHERE DO ANTS LIVE? Ants are social insects that live together in large groups, or colonies. Their group home is usually a system of underground tunnels and chambers, with mounds above formed out of the dirt or sand they removed in digging. But some ants are different. **Carpenter ants** carve tunnels in wood (but don't eat it). In the rain forests of South America, the **Aztec ant** lives inside trees. **Tailor ants** from the tropics of Africa use leaves to build their nests. And **Army ants** don't build at all. They travel in big groups looking for food.

DO ANTS HAVE JOBS? Each ant has a specific job. The **queen** lays eggs to populate the colony. **Workers** collect food, feed members of the colony, and enlarge the nest. **Soldiers** are large workers that defend the colony and sometimes attack ants who are strangers. All these hard-working ants are female. **Males** have wings to fly to another colony, where they mate with a queen and die soon afterwards.

WHAT DO ANTS EAT? Ants are very fond of eating sweet foods, seeds, and other insects. Sweets provide energy for worker ants, and the protein from other insects helps build up the ant's body. The **Dalmatie ant** actually cooks its food by chewing it into patties and baking them in the sun. **Harvester ants** collect and store seeds. **Leaf-cutter ants** grow fungus for food.

HOW DO ANTS COMMUNICATE? Ants communicate by touching each other with their antennae. They show other ants where food is by making a path with a chemical (called a pheromone) that leaves a scent that the ants follow.

The world's biggest ant colony was discovered in 2002. This supercolony has billions of ants living in millions of nests. It stretches 3,600 miles, all the way from Italy to northwest Spain.

QUESTIONS TO PONDER

1. Are all soldier ants male or female?

2. On which continent is the world's biggest ant colony located?

    a. Asia   b. Spain   c. Europe

3. An ant can lift 50 times its own weight. If someone who weighed 82 pounds could do that, how much could that person lift?

4. Can you think of ways it would be better—and ways it would be worse—if people were more like ants?

Dangerous Animals

What's the difference between poisonous animals and venomous animals? Poisonous animals contain a toxin (poison) in a part of their body, like the skin, organs, or feathers. Touching or eating these animals causes sickness, pain, or death. But, these animals don't do anything to spread their poison. Venomous animals do deliver their poison. They use body parts such as fangs, stingers, or tentacles to do this.

Here are some kinds of poisonous or venomous animals:

► **Black widow** spiders are armed with venom that is 15 times more poisonous than the venom of a prairie rattlesnake. They are found in warm and temperate climates around the world and like to live in dark places such as drain pipes and under rocks and logs. Their bite rarely kills humans. Why do we call them the black widow? Because the female sometimes eats the smaller male after mating!

► The **blue ring octopus**, the deadliest kind of octopus, uses its arms to capture its prey. Then it bites the victim, sending in a poison through its saliva strong enough to kill a human.

► Although its name means "100 legs," the common **centipede** is about 2 inches long with only 15 pairs of legs. Centipedes eat insects, earthworms, spiders, slugs, and some small animals. They move fast and use venom, which comes from glands near the first pair of legs, to kill their prey. Although their bite can be painful to humans, it is not deadly.

► The largest venomous snake, the **king cobra**, uses its half-inch-long hollow fangs to inject its prey with toxin (poison) strong enough to kill an elephant. King cobras mainly eat lizards and other snakes.

► **Komodo dragons'** mouths are full of disease-causing bacteria. When they bite their prey, the victim gets sick and slowly dies of blood poisoning. Then the lizard returns to eat the body.

► The skin glands of **poison dart frogs** produce a foul-smelling, bitter-tasting substance that warns away predators. A single drop can kill an animal that ignores the warning. People can get sick from touching the frog's skin. In Colombia, people have used the toxin in hunting darts (blowguns).

► The skin, liver, and eggs of the **puffer fish** contain deadly toxins. Some chefs in Japan are trained and licensed to prepare a special treat made out of puffers. The chefs are usually able to make this dish safely. But not always. At least a few people die each year from eating it.

► **Scorpions** have eight legs and a hard outer skeleton like spiders and ticks. They live in nearly every type of habitat, including deserts, rain forests, prairies, grasslands, forests, mountains, caves, ponds, and the seashore. The stinger at the tip of their tails injects a paralyzing poison into their prey. The sting of most scorpions is only irritating to people, but there are about 25 species of scorpions that can kill a person.

► Although **sea anemones** look like beautiful flowers attached to coral or rocks on the ocean floor, they are actually predatory animals. The sea anemone's tentacles are studded with microscopic stinging capsules to protect it and catch its food. Sea anemones have few enemies and live a long time.

━━━ QUESTIONS TO PONDER ━━━

1. What does the word "centipede" mean?
2. True or False: Komodo dragons kill their prey by biting it several times until it dies.
3. Where does the name "poison dart frogs" come from?
4. Why do you think people would be willing to eat a puffer fish when they know it can be poisonous? Would you ever try such a delicacy?

Musical Instruments

There are many kinds of musical instruments. Instruments in an orchestra are divided into four groups, or sections: percussion, woodwind, brass, and string.

PERCUSSION INSTRUMENTS make sounds when they are struck. This group includes drums, cymbals, triangles, gongs, bells, and xylophones. Keyboard instruments, like the piano, are sometimes thought of as percussion instruments.

WOODWINDS are long and round and hollow inside. They make sounds when air is blown into them through a mouth hole or a reed. The clarinet, flute, oboe, bassoon, and piccolo are woodwinds.

BRASSES are hollow inside. They make sounds when air is blown into a mouthpiece shaped like a cup or a funnel. The trumpet, French horn, trombone, and tuba are brasses.

STRINGED INSTRUMENTS make sounds when the strings are either stroked with a bow or plucked with the fingers. The violin, viola, cello, bass, and harp are used in an orchestra. The guitar, banjo, and mandolin are other stringed instruments.

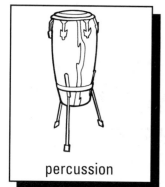  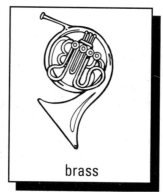 

percussion   woodwind   brass   string

Did You Know?

A person's voice can be considered his or her instrument. Human voices have a range in pitch from low to high. For men, the low end is called the bass (pronounced like base), followed by baritone and tenor. The range for women goes from contralto (the lowest) up to alto, mezzo-soprano, and soprano.

QUESTIONS TO PONDER

1. What kind of instrument is an oboe?

    a. string   b. woodwind   c. percussion

2. What kind of instrument is a xylophone?

    a. string   b. woodwind   c. percussion

3. Each of the following words is broken into two-letter sections. If you rearrange the letters, which one names a stringed instrument?

    a. IN MA ND OL   b. IN AR ET CL   c. BO TR OM NE

4. If you could be a great musician on one instrument, which would it be? Why?

Through Artists' Eyes

Artists look at the world in a new way. Their work can be funny or sad, beautiful or disturbing, real-looking or strange.

Throughout history, artists have painted pictures of nature (called landscapes), or pictures of people (called portraits), or pictures of flowers in vases, food, and other objects (known as still lifes).

► Many artists still paint these kinds of pictures. But some artists today create pictures that do not look like anything in the real world. These paintings are examples of **abstract art**, or modern art.

► **Photography,** too, may be a form of art. Photos record both the commonplace and the exotic, and help us look at events in new ways.

► **Sculpture** is a three dimensional form made from clay, stone, metal, or other material. Many sculptures stand freely so that you can walk around them. Some are mobiles that hang from the ceiling. Sculptures can be large, like the Statue of Liberty, or small. Some sculptures are real-looking. Others have no form that can be recognized.

In 1962 illustrator Andy Warhol became famous for his paintings of Campbell's Soup cans.

QUESTIONS TO PONDER

1. What are paintings of people called?

2. Which type of art form is the Statue of Liberty?

3. Paintings of pictures that do not look like anything in the real world are considered to be .

   a. still lifes   b. abstract art   c. landscapes

4. Do you think paintings of commonplace objects such as soup cans should be considered art? Why or why not?

The World of Books

There are so many types of books to read and enjoy! Here are a few different categories of books and examples of the books that fit in each category.

Fiction

The Chronicles of Narnia by C.S. Lewis.

Secret passages lead four children to Narnia, a land of talking animals, evil witches, wicked dragons, magic spells, and amazing adventures. *The Lion, the Witch, and the Wardrobe* was first in the series.

A Wrinkle in Time by Madeleine L'Engle.

Meg Murray travels through space with her brother and friend to find her father, a scientist who disappeared while working on a secret government project.

Nonfiction

Machu Picchu by Elizabeth Mann.

The incredible story of the Incas and the breathtaking city they built high in the Andes Mountains.

So, You Want to Be President? by Judith St. George; illustrated by David Small.

This book captures the funny, personal side of the presidents' lives.

Poetry

The Gargoyle on the Roof by Jack Prelutsky; illustrated by Peter Sis.

Illustrated poems about werewolves, vampires, trolls, gremlins, and other scary creatures.

Remember the Bridge: Poems of a People by Carole Boston Weatherford.

Poems and photos celebrating 400 years of African-American heroes.

Reference

Almanac: An annual one-volume book of facts and statistics.

Atlas: A collection of maps.

Dictionary: A book of words in alphabetical order. It gives meanings and spellings and shows how words are pronounced.

Encyclopedia: A place to go for information on almost any subject.

QUESTIONS TO PONDER

1. In which reference book would you look if you wanted to find out how to pronounce the word *gargoyle*?

2. In which category would *Harry Potter and the Sorcerer's Stone* fit?

    a. fiction   b. nonfiction   c. poetry

3. In which mountain range would you find the city of Machu Picchu?

4. Which type of book do you most enjoy reading: fiction, nonfiction, or poetry? Why do you think you enjoy that particular type of book the most?

Computer Basics

If your family owns a home computer, you probably use it to do all kinds of things. You might spend hours each day playing the latest computer game or sending instant messages to your friends. Or you might even use your computer to word process a report for homework. Either way, your computer performs each of these functions perfectly and in no time at all. How does it do that?

For a computer to do its work, every piece of information given to it must be translated into binary code. You are probably used to using 10 digits, 0 through 9, when you do arithmetic. When the computer uses the binary code, it uses only two digits, 0 and 1. Think of it as sending messages to the computer by switching a light on and off.

Each 0 or 1 digit is called a bit, and most computers use a sequence of 8 bits (called a byte) for each piece of data. Almost all computers use the same code, called ASCII (pronounced "askey"), to stand for letters of the alphabet, number digits, punctuation, and other special characters that control the computer's operation. Below is a list of ASCII bytes for the alphabet.

A 01000001	H 01001000	O 01001111	U 01010101
B 01000010	I 01001001	P 01010000	V 01010110
C 01000011	J 01001010	Q 01010001	W 01010111
D 01000100	K 01001011	R 01010010	X 01011000
E 01000101	L 01001100	S 01010011	Y 01011001
F 01000110	M 01001101	T 01010100	Z 01011010
G 01000111	N 01001110		

RAM, or random access memory, is the memory your computer uses to open programs and store your work until you save it to the hard drive or a disk. The information in RAM disappears when the computer is turned off. ROM, or read only memory, contains permanent instructions for the computer and cannot be changed. The information in ROM remains after the computer is turned off.

QUESTIONS TO PONDER

1. Which contains your computer's permanent instructions: RAM or ROM?

2. How would you spell the word "cat" in binary code?

3. If 8 bits equal 1 byte, then how many bits would there be in 12 bytes?

4. Can you think of other words that start with the prefix *bi-*? What do most of these words have in common?

The Origins of Computers

The high-speed computers we have now would never have been possible without the original inventions that came before them. Here are two stories of machines that would look very primitive to us but proved very important to the modern-day computers we now depend on.

Charles Babbage and His Difference Engine

In the 1820s, Englishman Charles Babbage designed a mechanical device he called a **difference engine**. He designed it to do simple math, but he never could finish building it because it was so expensive and complicated. One hundred and seventy years later, though, scientists used Babbage's drawings to build his machine, and guess what? It worked perfectly! Babbage's difference engine is the great-grandfather of today's calculators and computers.

All About ENIAC

During World War II, a team at the University of Pennsylvania's Computing Lab was helping the Army with calculations for its artillery, but couldn't keep up with the demand. Then two leaders of the team, John Mauchley and Presper Eckert, got an idea. How about building an automatic calculating machine? The result was a huge contraption that stood 10 feet tall, weighed 30 tons, and filled a 50 by 30 ft room. Known as the ENIAC, or Electronic Numerical Integrator and Computer, it used 18,000 vacuum tubes and 6,000 switches to churn out answers. ENIAC was 1,000 times faster than the best calculating machine before it, but no match for today's computers. A computer's speed is often measured in MIPS (millions of instructions per second). ENIAC could execute 0.05 MIPS. A modern computer, with a 1.5 GHz Pentium 4 processor, can perform about 1,700 MIPS.

— QUESTIONS TO PONDER —

1. What does ENIAC stand for?

2. Why didn't Charles Babbage build his difference engine?

3. In what decade did scientists use Babbage's drawings to build his machine?

4. How would your life be different if there were no computers? Give three examples.

The Internet

What Is the Internet?

The Internet ("Net") connects computers from around the world so people can share information. You can play games on the Net, send e-mail, shop, and find information. By using a program called a **browser**, you can get onto the **World Wide Web (www)**, which lets you see information using pictures, colors, and sounds. Information on the Web lives on a **Web site**. To get to the Web site you want, you need to use the right **Universal Resource Locator (URL)**, or address. If you know the address, just find the place for it on the screen and type it in carefully.

If you don't know the address, hit **Search**. You may have to pick a **search engine**, which is like a huge index. A few popular search engines are Yahoo, Google, and Lycos. When you have the one you want, type in words that tell what you're searching for. You will get a list of sites. You can choose the site most likely to have the information you want. Some sites have **links**—names of other sites on the same subject.

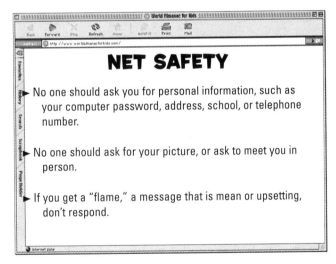

Can you depend on information from the Internet?

Watch out when you use information from the Internet. The source may not be reliable. An official Web site produced by a company, organization, or government agency may be more reliable than a site created by a fan. Librarians can often give good advice about sites. And it often may be worth checking more than one source.

QUESTIONS TO PONDER

1. What does "URL" stand for?

2. Which of the following helps you get onto the World Wide Web?

   a. search engine   b. browser   c. links

3. What information should you not share with strangers on the Net?

4. What are some ways, if any, that you or your family uses the Internet?

Energy Keeps Us Moving

You can't touch, see, smell, or taste energy, but you can observe what it does. You can feel that sunlight warms objects, and you can see that electricity lights up a light bulb, even if you can't see the heat or the electricity.

What Is Energy?—Things that you see and touch every day use some form of energy to work: your body, a bike, a basketball, a car. Energy enables things to move. Scientists define energy as the ability to do work.

Why Do We Need Energy to Do Work?—Scientists define work as a force moving an object. Scientifically speaking, throwing a ball is work, but studying for a test isn't! When you throw a ball, you use energy from the food you eat to do work on the ball. The engine in a car uses energy from gasoline to make the car move.

Are There Different Kinds of Energy?

POTENTIAL—When we rest or sleep we still have the ability to move. We do not lose our energy. We simply store it for another time. Stored energy is called potential energy. When we get up and begin to move around, we are using stored energy.	**KINETIC**—As we move around and walk, our stored (potential) energy changes into kinetic energy, which is the energy of moving things. A parked car has potential energy. A moving car has kinetic energy. A sled stopped at the top of the hill has potential energy. As the sled goes down the hill, its potential energy changes to kinetic energy.

How Is Energy Created?—Energy cannot be created or destroyed, but it can be changed or converted into different forms. Heat, light, and electricity are all forms of energy. Other forms of energy are sound, chemical energy, mechanical energy, and nuclear energy.

Where Does Energy Come From?—All of the forms of energy we use come from the energy stored in natural resources. Sunlight, water, wind, petroleum, coal, and natural gas are natural resources. From these resources, we get heat and electricity.

QUESTIONS TO PONDER

1. What is another name for stored energy?

2. How do scientists define work?

3. Explain how a bicycle has both potential energy and kinetic energy.

4. Make two lists, one called "Potential Energy" and the other called "Kinetic Energy." Now look around your classroom. Try to find at least five items for each list. Which list was easier to fill? Why?

Energy from the Sun

All of our energy comes from the sun. Inside the sun, hydrogen atoms join together and become helium. This process releases energy that radiates into space in the form of waves. These waves give us heat and light. Energy from the sun is stored in our food and provides fuel for our bodies. Some of the energy from the sun is stored in the form of fossil fuels.

Plants absorb energy from the Sun (solar energy) and convert absorbed energy to chemical energy for storage.

Animals eat plants and gain the stored chemical energy.

Food provides the body with energy to work and play.

People eat plants and meat.

Long before humans existed, trees and other plants absorbed the sun's energy. Animals ate plants and smaller animals. After the plants and animals died, they got buried deeper and deeper underground. After millions of years, they turned into coal and petroleum—fossil fuels.

Solar cars don't have gas tanks. Instead, they have panels of solar cells—small wafer-like units that change light into electrical energy.

Engineers test their latest models by racing them. The 1,800-mile World Solar Challenge in Australia, which began in 1987, is the oldest solar race. In 2001, this race even included solar motorcycles! A Dutch team won, setting a record of 32 hours, 39 minutes—an average of 57 mph.

Engineers admit that solar cars won't replace gas-powered cars any time soon. The big challenge is to design a battery that can store enough energy to keep the car running when the sun isn't shining.

QUESTIONS TO PONDER

1. Finish this sentence: Solar cars don't have _____.

   a. tires   b. gas tanks   c. batteries

2. Which of the following isn't a fossil fuel?

   a. coal   b. petroleum   c. helium

3. What objects on Earth absorb solar energy and convert it into chemical energy?

4. Design and draw a solar-powered car. Be sure to include lots of space for solar panels.

Sources of Energy

Read the information over the next two pages to find out more about the types of energy that are available on Earth.

FOSSIL FUELS

Fuels are called "fossil" if they were formed from ancient plants and animals. The three basic fossil fuels are **coal**, **oil**, and **natural gas**. Most of the energy we use today comes from these sources. **Coal** is mined, either at the surface or deep underground. **Oil**, or petroleum, is a liquid that is removed by drilling wells. **Natural gas**, which is made up mostly of a gas called methane, also comes from wells. Natural gas is a clean-burning fuel, and it is being used more and more. Oil and coal bring a greater risk of air pollution.

All fossil fuels have one problem: they are gradually getting used up. There are special problems about oil, because industrial countries must often import lots of it and can become greatly dependent on other countries for their supply.

NUCLEAR ENERGY

Nuclear power is created by releasing energy stored in the nucleus of an atom. This process is nuclear **fission**, which is also called "splitting" an atom. Fission takes place in a **reactor**, which allows the nuclear reaction to be controlled. Nuclear power plants release almost no air pollution. Many countries today use nuclear energy.

Nuclear power does cause some safety concerns. In 1979 there was a nuclear accident at Three Mile Island in Pennsylvania that led to the release of some radiation. A much more serious accident occurred at Chernobyl in Ukraine in 1986. An explosion there killed about 8,000 people, and a wide area was exposed to dangerous radiation.

WATER POWER

Water power is energy that comes from the force of falling or fast-flowing water. It was put to use early in human history. **Water wheels**, turned by rivers or streams, were common in the Middle Ages. They were used for tasks like grinding grain and sawing lumber.

Today, water power comes from waterfalls or from specially built dams. As water flows from a higher to a lower level, it runs a turbine—a device that turns an electric generator. This is called **hydroelectric power** (hydro = water). Today, over half of the world's hydroelectric power is produced in five countries: Brazil, Russia, Canada, China, and the United States.

SOLAR POWER

Energy directly from sunlight is a promising new technology. Vast amounts of this energy falls upon the Earth every day—and it is not running out. Energy from the sun is expected to run for some 5 billion years. Solar energy is also friendly to the environment. One drawback is space. To get enough light, the surfaces that gather solar energy need to be spread out a lot. Also, the energy can't be gathered when the sun isn't shining.

A solar cell is usually made of silicon, a **semiconductor**. That means it can change sunlight into electricity. The cost of solar cells has been dropping in recent years. Large plants using solar-cell systems have been built in several countries, including Japan, Saudi Arabia, the United States, and Germany.

Sources of Energy *(cont.)*

GEOTHERMAL ENERGY

Geothermal energy is heat from the Earth. About 30 miles below the surface is a layer called the **mantle**. This is the source of the gas and lava that erupts from volcanoes. Hot springs and geysers, with temperatures as high as 700 degrees, are also heated by the mantle. Because it's so hot, the mantle holds great promise as an energy source, especially in areas where the hot water is close to the surface. Iceland, which has many active volcanoes and hot springs, uses lots of geothermal energy. About 85% of homes there are heated this way.

BIOMASS ENERGY

Burning wood and straw (materials known as **biomass**) is probably the oldest way of producing energy. It's an old idea, but it still has value. Researchers are growing crops to use as fuel. Biomass fuels can be burned, like coal, in a power plant. They can also be used to make **ethanol**, which is similar to gasoline. Most ethanol comes from corn, which can make it expensive. But researchers are experimenting with other crops, like "switchgrass" and alfalfa.

Recently, a biomass power plant was opened in Burlington, Vermont. It turns wood chips, solid waste, and switchgrass into a substance similar to natural gas.

WIND ENERGY

People have used wind as energy for a long time. **Windmills** were popular in Europe during the Middle Ages. Today, huge high-tech windmills with propeller-like blades are grouped together in **"wind farms."** Dozens of wind turbines are spaced well apart (so they don't block each other's wind). Even on big wind farms, the windmills usually take up less than 1% of the ground space. The rest of the land can still be used for farming or for grazing animals.

Wind power is a rapidly growing technology that doesn't pollute or get used up like fossil fuels. In 2001, there was four times as much electricity generated by wind as there had been in 1996. Unfortunately, the generators only work if the wind blows.

QUESTIONS TO PONDER

1. In which country are 85% of the homes heated by geothermal energy?

2. What is the process of "splitting" an atom called?

3. Give two main drawbacks to using fossil fuels for energy.

4. What are some ways your town could replace the use of fossil fuels with cleaner forms of energy? What are some drawbacks of using these different types of energy?

Producers and Consumers

The United States produces about 19 percent of the world's energy—more than any other country—but it uses 25 percent of the world's energy. The table on the left lists the world's top ten energy-producers and the percent of the world's production that each was responsible for in 1999. The other table lists the world's top energy-users and the percent of the world's energy use that each was responsible for.

Countries That Produce the Most Energy	
United States	19 percent
Russia	11 percent
China	8 percent
Saudi Arabia	5 percent
Canada	5 percent
Great Britain	3 percent
Iran	3 percent
Norway	3 percent
India	2 percent
Mexico	2 percent

Countries That Consume the Most Energy	
United States	25 percent
China	9 percent
Russia	7 percent
Japan	6 percent
Germany	4 percent
Canada	3 percent
India	3 percent
France	3 percent
Great Britain	3 percent
Brazil	2 percent

Where Does Our Energy Come From?

In 2000, most of the energy used in the United States came from fossil fuels (almost 39% from petroleum, 23% from natural gas, and 22% from coal). The rest came mostly from hydropower (water power), nuclear energy, and renewable resources such as geothermal, solar, and wind energy, and from burning materials such as wood and animal waste.

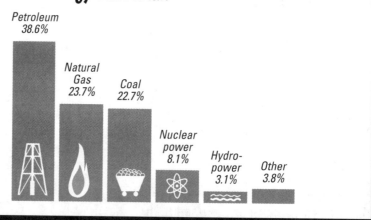

Petroleum 38.6%
Natural Gas 23.7%
Coal 22.7%
Nuclear power 8.1%
Hydro-power 3.1%
Other 3.8%

QUESTIONS TO PONDER

1. What is hydropower?

2. Which of the following countries produces a higher percentage of the world's energy than it consumes?

   a. China   b. Iran   c. India

3. According to the bar graph above, what is the exact percentage of U.S. energy that comes from fossil fuels?

   a. 85%   b. 62.3%   c. 46.4%

4. Do you think the U.S. consumes too much energy? If your answer is yes, then what are some ways in which the U.S. can consume less energy? If no, then why do you think the U.S. deserves to consume ¼ of the world's energy?

Biomes

A biome is a large natural area that is the home to a certain type of plant. The animals, climate, soil, and even the amount of water in the region also help distinguish a biome. The are more than 30 kinds of biomes in the world. The following five types cover most of Earth's surface:

❶ FORESTS

Forests cover about ⅓ of Earth's land surface. There are a few different types of forests. Furthest from the equator are evergreen forests. These are cool in temperature and contain trees such as pines, firs, and spruces. Temperate forests are a little closer to the equator and have warm, rainy summers and cold, snowy winters. Here deciduous trees (which lose their leaves in the fall and grow new ones in the spring) join the evergreens. Near the equator are tropical rain forests, home to the greatest variety of plants on Earth. The temperature never falls below freezing except on the mountain slopes. These forests receive a lot of rainfall, and the trees stay green all year.

❷ TUNDRA AND ALPINE REGION

In the northernmost regions of North America, Europe, and Asia surrounding the Arctic Ocean are plains called the tundra. The temperature rarely rises above 45°F (7°C), and it is too cold for trees to grow there. Most tundra plants are mosses and lichens that hug the ground for warmth. This type of climate and plant life also exists in the alpine regions, on top of the world's highest mountains (such as the Himalayas, Alps, Andes, and Rockies).

❸ DESERTS

The driest areas of the world are the deserts. They can be hot or cold, but they also contain an amazing number of plants. Cactuses and sagebrush are native to dry regions of North and South America. Dates have grown in the deserts of the Middle East and Africa for thousands of years.

❹ GRASSLANDS

The areas of the world that are too dry to have green forests but not dry enough for deserts are called grasslands. The most common plants found there are grasses. The drier grasslands are used for grazing cattle and sheep. In the prairies, where there is a little more rain, important grains such as wheat, rye, and barley are grown.

❺ OCEANS

Covering ⅔ of Earth, the ocean is by far the largest biome. Within the ocean are smaller biomes that include coastal areas, tidal zones, and coral reefs. Reefs are called the "rainforests of the ocean." Australia's Great Barrier Reef is the largest in the world.

━━━━━━━ QUESTIONS TO PONDER ━━━━━━━

1. What are deciduous trees?

2. What are often called the "rainforest of the ocean"?

       a. tidal zones   b. coral reefs   c. grasslands

3. If you were a farmer who raised livestock for a living, which of the five biomes listed would you most likely live in?

4. Which biome best describes the area in which you live? Give a few reasons to support your answer.

Threats to the Environment

AIR POLLUTION

Air pollution is a dirtying of the air caused by toxic chemicals or other materials. The major sources of air pollution are cars, trucks and buses, waste incinerators, factories, and some electric power plants, especially those that burn fossil fuels, such as coal.

Because air is so basic to life, it is very important to keep the air clean by reducing or preventing air pollution. Air pollution causes lots of health problems and may help bring about acid rain, global warming, and a breakdown of the ozone layer.

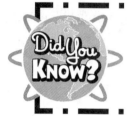

The air we breathe is made up mainly of gases: around 78% nitrogen, 21% oxygen, and 1% carbon dioxide, water vapor, and other gases. Humans breathe more than six quarts of air every minute.

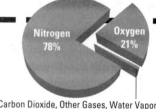

Carbon Dioxide, Other Gases, Water Vapor 1%

ACID RAIN

Acid rain is polluted rain or other precipitation that results from chemicals released into the air. The main sources of these chemicals are fumes, cars' exhaust pipes, and power plants that burn coal. When these chemicals mix with moisture and other particles, they create sulfuric acid and nitric acid. Winds often carry these acids many miles before they drop down in rain, snow, and fog, or even as dry particles. Acid rain can cause our eyes to sting and even make some people sick. It can also harm crops and trees.

GLOBAL WARMING

The Earth's climate is gradually become warmer. Four of the six hottest years on record have occurred since 1997. If the climate becomes too warm, lots of ice near the North and South Poles could melt. More water would go into the oceans, and many areas along the coasts could be flooded.

What is causing this global warming? In Earth's atmosphere, there are tiny amounts of gases that allow heat from the sun to pass through but then hold it in as it comes up from the sun-warmed Earth—in much the same way as the glass walls of a greenhouse hold in the warmth of the sun. Many of the same things that cause air pollution—cars, factories, etc.—also release more of these greenhouse gases into the atmosphere. This causes more heat to be trapped inside Earth's atmosphere. It is called the greenhouse effect.

DEFORESTATION

Trees and forests are very important to the environment. They use carbon dioxide and give off oxygen, which animals and plants need for survival. They also hold water and provide homes and food for millions of types of animals. Cutting down many trees is called *deforestation*, and it can have serious effects. Animals and plants are affected, an area's climate can be altered, and soil can erode.

QUESTIONS TO PONDER

1. What percentage of the air we breathe is oxygen?
2. What gas do trees use, and what gas do they give off?
3. If four of the six hottest years on record have occurred since 1997, what percentage of the six hottest years have occurred since 1997?
4. Most threats to the environment are brought on by people. What are some ways that you can help contribute to a healthier environment?

Water, Water Everywhere

Earth is the water planet. More than ⅔ of its surface is covered with water, and every living thing on it needs water to live. Water is not only part of our life (cooking, cleaning, bathing), it's about 75% of our brains and 60% of our whole bodies!

HOW MUCH IS THERE TO DRINK? Seawater makes up 97% of the world's water. Another 2% of the water is frozen in ice caps, icebergs, glaciers, and sea ice. Half of the 1% left is too far underground to be reached. That leaves only 0.5% of freshwater for all the people, plants, and animals on Earth. This supply is renewable only by rainfall.

WHERE DOES DRINKING WATER COME FROM? Most smaller cities and towns get their freshwater from groundwater—melted snow and rain that seeps deep into the ground and is drawn out from wells. Larger cities usually rely on lakes or reservoirs for their water. Some areas of the world with little fresh water are turning to a process called **desalinization** (removing salt from seawater) as a solution. There is plenty of salt water to go around, but this process is slow and expensive.

THE HYDROLOGICAL CYCLE: WATER'S ENDLESS JOURNEY
Water is special. It's the only thing on Earth that exists naturally in all three physical states: solid (ice), liquid, and gas (water vapor). It never boils naturally (except around volcanoes), but it evaporates (turns into a gas) easily into the air. These unique properties send water on a cycle of repeating events.

HOW DOES WATER GET INTO THE AIR? Sunlight causes surface water in oceans, lakes, swamps, and rivers to turn into water vapor. This is called **evaporation**. Plant photosynthesis releases water vapor into the air. Animals also release a little bit when they breathe. This is **transpiration**.

HOW DOES WATER COME OUT OF THE AIR? Warm air holds more water vapor than cold air. As the air rises into the atmosphere, it cools and the water vapor **condenses**—changes back into a tiny water droplets. These form clouds. As the drops get bigger, gravity pulls them down as **precipitation** (rain, snow, sleet, fog, and dew are all types of precipitation).

WHERE DOES THE WATER GO? Depending on where the precipitation lands, it can: **1.** evaporate back into the atmosphere; **2.** run off into streams and rivers; **3.** be absorbed by plants; **4.** soak down into the soil as ground water; **5.** fall as snow on a glacier and be trapped as ice for thousands of years.

QUESTIONS TO PONDER

1. Which holds more water vapor: warm air or cold air?

2. What is the process of removing salt from salt water called?
   a. desalinization   b. evaporation   c. desalting

3. Sixty percent of a person's body weight is water. If a person weighs 150 pounds, about how many pounds of his or her weight is water?

4. Is there anything you can do to help keep the world's water supply from running out? Give five ways in which you can help to conserve water.

Where Garbage Goes

Most of the things around you will be replaced or thrown away someday. Skates, clothes, the toaster, furniture—they can break or wear out, or you may get tired of them. Where will they go when they are thrown out? What kinds of waste will they create, and how will it affect the environment?

What Happens to Things We Throw Away?

LANDFILLS

Most of our trash goes to places called landfills. A **landfill** (or dump) is a low area of land that is filled with garbage. Most modern landfills are lined with a layer of plastic or clay to try to keep dangerous liquids from seeping into the soil and ground water supply.

THE PROBLEM WITH LANDFILLS

More than half of the states in this country are running out of places to dump their garbage. Because of the unhealthful materials many contain, landfills do not make good neighbors, and people don't want to live near them. Many landfills are located in poor neighborhoods.

INCINERATORS

One way to get rid of trash is to burn it. Trash is burned in a furnace-like device called an **incinerator**. Because incinerators can get rid of almost all of the bulk of the trash, some communities would rather use incinerators than landfills.

THE PROBLEM WITH INCINERATORS

Leftover ash and smoke from burning trash may contain harmful chemicals, called **pollutants**, and make it hard for some people to breathe. They can harm plants, animals, and people.

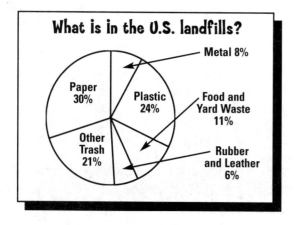

What is in the U.S. landfills?

Paper 30%
Plastic 24%
Metal 8%
Food and Yard Waste 11%
Rubber and Leather 6%
Other Trash 21%

Did You Know?

Every year on the third Saturday in September, the International Coastal Cleanup takes place along beaches, rivers, and waterways around the world. In 2000, 850,000 volunteers collected 13.5 million pounds of trash.

QUESTIONS TO PONDER

1. About what percentage of trash in U.S. landfills is either paper or plastic?

2. Of the following words, which is the best synonym for incinerate?

    a. pollute   b. recycle   c. burn

3. If 850,000 volunteers collected 13,500,000 million pounds of trash, about how many pounds of trash did each volunteer collect on average?

    a. 1.6 pounds   b. 16 pounds   c. 61 pounds

4. Now that you know the problems associated with landfills and incinerators, what do you think we should do with all of our trash?

Land and Water

Almost ⅔ of Earth's surface is made up of water. The rest is land. Oceans are the largest areas of water. Continents are the biggest pieces of land.

THE FOUR OCEANS

The facts about the oceans include their size and average depth.

PACIFIC OCEAN: 64,186,300 square miles; 12,925 feet deep
ATLANTIC OCEAN: 33,420,000 square miles; 11,730 feet deep
INDIAN OCEAN: 28,350,500 square miles; 12,598 feet deep
ARCTIC OCEAN: 5,105,700 square miles; 3,407 feet deep

Let's take a close look at the seven continents:

	Area	2001 Population	Highest Point	Lowest Point
North America	8,300,000 square miles	486,000,000	Mount McKinley (Alaska), 20,320 feet	Death Valley (California), 282 feet below sea level
South America	6,800,000 square miles	351,000,000	Mount Aconcagua (Argentina), 22,834 feet	Valdes Peninsula (Argentina), 131 feet below sea level
Europe	8,800,000 square miles	729,000,000	Mount Elbrus (Russia), 18,510 feet	Caspian Sea (Russia, Azerbaijan; eastern Europe and western Asia), 92 feet below sea level
Asia	12,000,000 square miles	3,737,000,000	Mount Everest (Nepal, Tibet), 29,035 feet	Dead Sea (Israel, Jordan), 1,312 feet below sea level
Africa	11,500,000 square miles	823,000,000	Mount Kilimanjaro (Tanzania), 19,340 feet	Lake Assal (Djibouti), 512 feet below sea level
Australia & Oceania	3,200,000 square miles	31,000,000	Mount Kosciusko (New South Wales), 7,310 feet	Lake Eyre (South Australia), 52 feet below sea level
Antarctica	5,400,000 square miles	No permanent residents	Vinson Massif, 16,864 feet	Bentley Subglacial Trench, 8,327 feet below sea level

QUESTIONS TO PONDER

1. Which continent is the least populated?

2. About how many Arctic Oceans could you fit into the Pacific Ocean? (*Round to the nearest number.*)

 a. 10   b. 13   c. 59

3. About how many people are there per square mile in Australia & Oceania?

 a. 10   b. 100   c. 1,000

4. Pretend that you wanted to climb from the highest elevation on Earth to the lowest elevation on Earth. Name the locations at which to begin and end.

Mapping the Earth

A globe is a small model of Earth. Like Earth, it is shaped like a ball or sphere. Earth isn't exactly a sphere because it gets flat at the top and bottom and bulges a little in the middle. This shape is called an oblate spheroid.

Because Earth is round, most flat maps that are centered on the equator do not show the shapes of the land masses exactly right. The shapes at the top and bottom usually look too big. For example, the island of Greenland, which is next to North America, may look bigger than Australia, though it is really much smaller.

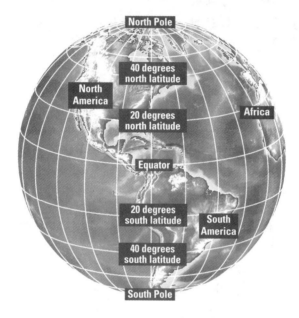

Draw an imaginary line around the middle of Earth. This is the **equator**. It splits Earth into two halves called hemispheres. The part north of the equator, including North America, is the northern hemisphere. The part south of the equator is the southern hemisphere.

You can also divide Earth into east and west. North and South America are in the western hemisphere. Africa, Asia, and most of Europe are in the eastern hemisphere.

═══ QUESTIONS TO PONDER ═══

1. What is the name of the imaginary line that splits Earth into two halves?

     a. the prime meridian   b. the hemisphere line   c. the equator

2. What is the technical term for the shape of the Earth?

3. Which two continents are in the Western Hemisphere?

     a. North America & Asia   b. North & South America   c. Africa & Asia

4. On a globe, find one country that is located on the equator.

Reading a Map

Below is a map of an imaginary place. Would you be able to find your way around if you went there?

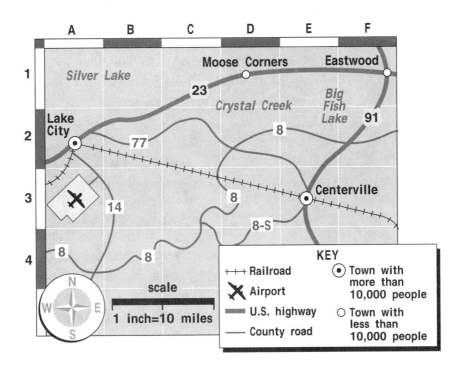

Maps can help you with . . .

✧ **Direction:** Maps usually have a compass rose that shows which way is north (N). When north is up on a map—as it is in this case—south (S) is down, east (E) is right, and west (W) is left.

✧ **Distance:** The scale shows you how to estimate the real distance between places on a map.

✧ **Symbols:** Maps usually have little pictures or symbols. The key tells you what those symbols mean.

✧ **Finding Places:** In the map above, you can find Centerville (E3) by drawing a straight line down from the letter E on top, and another line going across from the number 3 on the side. Lines made like this form a grid.

━━━ QUESTIONS TO PONDER ━━━

1. What feature on a map shows you which way is north?

2. Where on the map is Moose Corners?

    a. C1   b. D1   c. E1

3. Of the following numbers, which could be the population of Centerville.

    a. 1,101   b. 9,696   c. 13,899

4. On the back of your paper, draw a map of your classroom. Start by drawing a grid, as on the example above. Be sure to include a compass rose and a key to show symbols representing the different features in your classroom.

Volcanoes

A volcano is a mountain or hill with an opening on top known as a crater. Hot melted rock (magma), gases, ash, and other material from inside Earth mix together a few miles underground, rising up through cracks and weak spots in the mountain. Every once in a while, the mixture may blast out, or erupt, through the crater. The magma is called lava when it reaches the air. This red-hot lava may have a temperature of more than 2,000 degrees Fahrenheit. The hill or mountain is made of lava and other materials that come out of the opening, and then cool off and harden.

Some islands are really the tops of undersea volcanoes. The Hawaiian islands developed when volcanoes erupted under the Pacific Ocean.

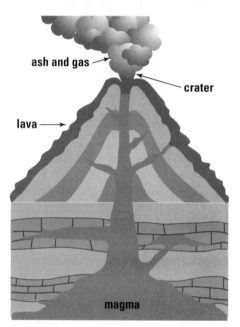

SOME FAMOUS VOLCANIC ERUPTIONS

Year	Volcano (place)	Deaths (approximate)
79	Mount Vesuvius (Italy)	16,000
1586	Kelut (Indonesia)	10,000
1792	Mount Unzen (Japan)	14,500
1815	Tambora (Indonesia)	10,000
1883	Krakatau or Krakatoa (Indonesia)	36,000
1902	Mount Pelée (Martinique)	28,000
1980	Mount St. Helens (U.S.)	57
1982	El Chichón (Mexico)	1,880
1985	Nevado del Ruiz (Colombia)	23,000
1986	Lake Nyos (Cameroon)	1,700
1991	Mt. Pinatubo (Philippines)	800

ICELAND *is the "Land of Fire and Ice." The island nation, about the size of Ohio, was formed by lava flows from its many active volcanoes. In spite of all the volcanic heat, Iceland has the largest glaciers in Europe—covering 11% of the country.*

QUESTIONS TO PONDER

1. What is the opening at the top of a volcano called?

2. About what percentage of Iceland is not covered with glaciers?

3. In the chart entitled "Some Famous Volcanic Eruptions," which is the only eruption listed that occurred on the continent of Europe?

    a. Mt. Vesuvius   b. Mt. St. Helens   c. Mt. Unzen

4. After Mount St. Helens erupted in 1980, many people decided to rebuild in the area near the volcano. Would you ever live near a volcano? Why or why not? Why do you think people were willing to take this risk again?

Earthquakes

Earthquakes may be so weak that they are hardly felt, or strong enough to do great damage. There are thousands of earthquakes each year, but most are too small to be noticed.

What Causes Earthquakes? Earth's outer layer, its crust, is divided into huge pieces called plates. These plates, made of rock, are constantly moving—away from each other, toward each other, or past each other. A crack in Earth's crust between two plates is called a fault. Many earthquakes occur along faults where two plates collide as they move toward each other or grind together as they move past each other.

Measuring Earthquakes The Richter scale goes from 0 to more than 8. These numbers indicate the strength of an earthquake. Each number means the quake releases about 30 times more energy than the number below it. An earthquake measuring 6 on the scale is about 30 times stronger than one measuring 5 and 900 times stronger than one measuring 4. Earthquakes that are 4 or above are considered major. (The damage and injuries caused by a quake also depend on other things, such as whether the area is heavily populated and built up.)

Magnitude	Effects
0-2	Earthquake is recorded by instruments but is not felt by people.
2-3	Earthquake is felt slightly by a few people.
3-4	People feel tremors; hanging objects like ceiling lights swing.
4-5	Earthquake causes some damage; walls crack; dishes and windows may break.
5-6	Furniture moves; earthquake seriously damages weak buildings.
6-7	Furniture may overturn; strong buildings are damaged; walls and buildings may collapse.
7-8	Many buildings are destroyed; underground pipes break; wide cracks appear in the ground.
ABOVE 8	Total devastation, including buildings and bridges; ground wavy.

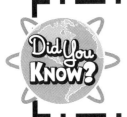

In 1906, a major earthquake destroyed much of the city of San Francisco. Many buildings in the city were built of wood, and fires set off by the earthquake burned almost 25,000 of them. No one knows exactly how many people were killed by the quake and fires, but it was probably more than 3,000.

═══ QUESTIONS TO PONDER ═══

1. What scale is used to measure earthquakes?

2. In 1906 a major earthquake destroyed which North American city?

3. If there is an earthquake measuring 4.7 on the Richter scale, which one of the following could be expected to happen?

   a. no damage at all   b. some minor damage   c. total destruction of homes

4. No one can predict when an earthquake will occur. What are some ways that you and your family can be prepared in case an earthquake strikes your city? What types of supplies would be valuable to have in case of an emergency?

We Are What We Eat

Have you ever noticed the labels on the packages of food you and your family buy? The labels provide information people need to make healthy choices about the foods they eat. Below are some terms you may see on labels.

NUTRIENTS ARE NEEDED

Nutrients are the parts of food the body can use. The body needs nutrients for growth, for energy, and to repair itself when something goes wrong. Carbohydrates, fats, proteins, vitamins, minerals, and water are different kinds of nutrients found in food. **Carbohydrates** and **fats** provide energy. **Proteins** aid growth and help maintain and repair the body. **Vitamins** help the body use food, help eyesight and skin, and aid in fighting off infections. **Minerals** help build bones and teeth and aid in such functions as muscle contractions and blood clotting. **Water** helps with growth and repair of the body. It also helps the body digest food and get rid of wastes.

CALORIES COUNT

A calorie is a measure of how much energy we get from food. The government recommends the number of calories that should be taken in for different age groups. The number of calories recommended for children ages 8 to 10 is about 1,900 a day. For ages 11 to 14, the government recommends around 2,200 calories a day for girls and 2,400 for boys.

To maintain a **healthy weight**, it is important to balance the calories in the food you eat with the calories used by the body every day. Every activity uses up some calories. The more active you are, the more calories your body burns. If you eat more calories than your body uses, you will gain weight.

Nutrition Facts

Serving Size 1/2 cup (1 oz.) = (30g)
Servings per container 14

Amount Per Serving	Cereal	Cereal w/ 1/2 cup Lowfat Milk
Calories	**100**	**150**
Calories from Fat	**10**	**25**
	% Daily Value**	
Total Fat 1g*	2%	4%
Saturated Fat 0g	0%	5%
Cholesterol 0mg	0%	3%
Sodium 50mg	2%	5%
Total Carbohydrates 20g	7%	9%
Dietary Fiber 2g	8%	8%
Sugars 5g		
Protein 4g		
Vitamin A	0%	6%
Vitamin C	0%	2%
Calcium	0%	15%
Iron	2%	4%

* Amount in Cereal. One half cup lowfat milk contributes an additional 50 calories, 1.5g total fat (1g saturated fat), 9 mg cholesterol, 60mg sodium, 6g total carbohydrates (6g sugars), and 3g protein.
** Percents (%) of a Daily Value are based on a 2,000 calorie diet. Your Daily Values may vary higher or lower depending on your calorie needs:

Nutrient	Calories	2,000	2,500
Total Fat	Less than	65g	80g
Sat Fat	Less than	20g	25g
Cholesterol	Less than	300mg	300mg
Sodium	Less than	2,400mg	2,400mg
Total Carbohydrates		300g	375g
Dietary Fiber		25g	30g

Calories per gram:
Fat 9 • Carbohydrate 4 • Protein 4

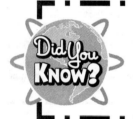

A little bit of fat is important for your body. It keeps your body warm. It gives the muscles energy. It helps keep the skin soft and healthy. But the body needs only a small amount of fat to do all these things. Less than ⅓ of your calories should come from fat if you're over two years old.

═══ QUESTIONS TO PONDER ═══

1. What do we call parts of food that a person's body can use?

2. Name two ways in which a little bit of fat in your diet can be helpful?

3. According to the food label on this page, how many calories are there in ¹/₂ cup of lowfat milk?

4. How aware are you of the amount of calories and nutrients you take in each day? Do you think you will be more concerned with nutrition when you get older? Why or why not?

The Importance of Exercise

Daily exercise makes you feel good. It also helps you think better, sleep better, feel more relaxed, and stay at a healthy weight. Regular exercise will make you stronger and help you improve at physical activities. About ¾ of ninth-graders say they get enough exercise. Do you?

Breathing deeply during exercise gets more oxygen into your lungs with each breath. Your heart pumps more oxygen-filled blood all through your body with each beat. Muscles and joints get stronger and more flexible as you use them.

Here are some activities, with a rough idea of how many calories a 100-pound person would burn per minute while doing them:

ACTIVITY	CALORIES PER MINUTE
Jogging (6 miles per hour)	8
Jumping rope (easy)	7
Playing basketball	7
Playing soccer	6
Bicycling (9.4 miles per hour)	5
Skiing (downhill)	5
Raking the lawn	4
Rollerblading (easy)	4
Walking (4 miles per hour)	4
Bicycling (5.5 miles per hour)	3
Swimming (25 yards per minute)	3
Walking (3 miles per hour)	3

A lot of people think that it is unsafe to swim within an hour after they've eaten. It's actually alright to go in the water after you eat. But remember that some of your blood goes to the stomach area to help you digest your meal—leaving less blood to carry oxygen to your muscles, brain, and other organs. So don't overdo it. With less oxygen getting to your muscles, you could tire more easily. On land, you can stop to rest, but if you're in water over your head you might get into trouble. Also, it's definitely not a good idea to eat or chew gum while swimming because you could choke.

QUESTIONS TO PONDER

1. Breathing deeply during exercise helps get more _____ into your lungs.

    a. blood   b. oxygen   c. oxygen-filled blood

2. If a 100-pound person played soccer for ½ an hour, about how many total calories would he or she burn?

3. What percentage of ninth graders say that they get enough exercise?

    a. 75%   b. 66%   c. 34%

4. Do you think you get enough exercise? Do you think most children do? What might you do to exercise more?

Your Body

Your body is made up of many different parts that work together every minute of every day and night. It is more amazing than any machine or computer. Even though everyone's body looks different outside, people have the same parts inside.

To the right is a diagram of some of our bodies' major organs.

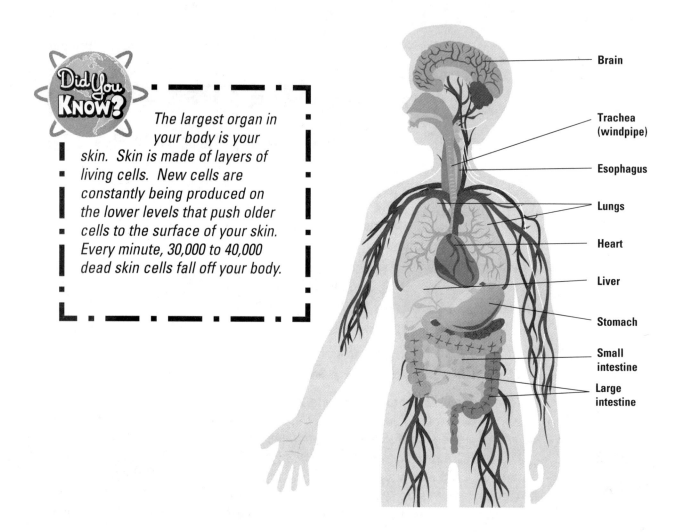

Did You KNOW?

The largest organ in your body is your skin. Skin is made of layers of living cells. New cells are constantly being produced on the lower levels that push older cells to the surface of your skin. Every minute, 30,000 to 40,000 dead skin cells fall off your body.

Brain

Trachea (windpipe)

Esophagus

Lungs

Heart

Liver

Stomach

Small intestine

Large intestine

BODY SYSTEMS

Each system of the body has its own job. Some of the systems also work together to keep you healthy and strong.

► **CIRCULATORY SYSTEM**—In the circulatory system, the **heart** pumps **blood**, which then travels through tubes, called **arteries**, to all parts of the body. The blood carries the oxygen and food that the body needs to stay alive. **Veins** carry the blood back to the heart.

► **DIGESTIVE SYSTEM**—The digestive system moves food through parts of the body called the **esophagus**, **stomach**, and **intestines**. As the food passes through, some of it is broken down into tiny particles called **nutrients**, which the body needs. Nutrients enter the bloodstream, which carries them to all parts of the body. The digestive system then changes the remaining food into waste that is eliminated from the body.

Your Body *(cont.)*

BODY SYSTEMS *(cont.)*

▶ **ENDOCRINE SYSTEM**—The endocrine system includes glands that are needed for some body functions. There are two kinds of glands. **Exocrine** glands produce liquids such as sweat and saliva. **Endocrine** glands produce chemicals called hormones. **Hormones** control body functions, such as growth.

▶ **MUSCULAR SYSTEM**—**Muscles** are made up of elastic fibers that help the body move. We use large muscles to walk and run, and small muscles to smile. Muscles also help protect organs.

▶ **SKELETAL SYSTEM**—The skeletal system is made up of the **bones** that hold your body upright. Some bones protect organs, such as the ribs that cover the lungs.

▶ **NERVOUS SYSTEM**—The nervous system enables us to think, feel, move, hear, and see. It includes the **brain**, the **spinal cord**, and **nerves** in all parts of the body. Nerves in the spinal cord carry signals back and forth between the brain and the rest of the body. The brain tells us what to do and how to respond. It has three major parts. The **cerebrum** controls thinking, speech, and vision. The **cerebellum** is responsible for physical coordination. The **brain stem** controls the respiratory, circulatory, and digestive systems.

▶ **RESPIRATORY SYSTEM**—The respiratory system allows us to breathe. Air comes into the body through the nose and mouth. It goes through the **windpipe** (or **trachea**) to two tubes (called **bronchi**), which carry air to the **lungs**. Oxygen from the air is taken in by tiny blood vessels in the lungs. The blood then carries oxygen to the cells of the body.

▶ **REPRODUCTIVE SYSTEM**—Through the reproductive system, adult human beings are able to create new human beings. Reproduction begins when a sperm cell from a man fertilizes an egg cell from a woman.

▶ **URINARY SYSTEM**—This system, which includes the **kidneys**, cleans waste from the blood and regulates the amount of water in the body.

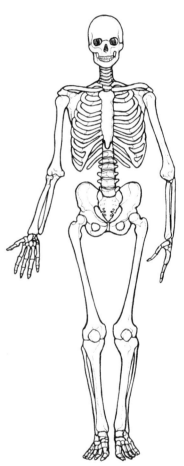

QUESTIONS TO PONDER

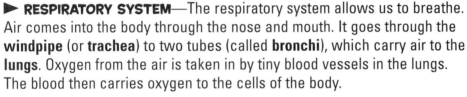

1. Which system of your body is mainly involved with eating and distributing nutrients?

2. What is falling off of your body, even at this very minute?

3. If a person suffered damage to his or her cerebellum, which of the following activities would most likely become more difficult for that person?

    a. reading a book   b. solving a math equation   c. climbing a ladder

4. Which body system are you most amazed by? Explain why.

Healthy Inventions

These days, people are living longer, healthier lives than ever before. These inventions are a few of the reasons why.

YEAR	Invention	Inventor (Country)
1752	lightning rod	Benjamin Franklin (U.S.)
1780	bifocal lenses for glasses	Benjamin Franklin (U.S.)
1815	safety lamp for miners	Sir Humphry Davy (England)
1819	stethoscope	René T.M.H. Laënnec (France)
1842	anesthesia (ether)	Crawford W. Long (U.S.)
1863	fire extinguisher	Alanson Crane (U.S.)
1895	X-ray	Wilhelm Roentgen (Germany)
1922	insulin	Sir Frederick G. Banting (Canada)
1923	automatic traffic signal	Garrett A. Morgan (U.S.)
1929	penicillin	Alexander Fleming (Scotland)
1952	airbag	John Hetrick (U.S.)
1954	antibiotic for fungal diseases	R. F. Brown & E. L. Hazen (U.S.)
1955	polio vaccine	Jonas E. Salk (U.S.)
1969	battery operated smoke detector	Randolph Smith & Kenneth House (U.S.)
1973	CAT scanner	Godfrey N. Hounsfield (England)
1978	artificial heart	Robert K. Jarvik (U.S.)
1987	meningitis vaccine	Connaught Lab (U.S.)

Scottish scientist Alexander Fleming was doing research on staphylococcus bacteria in 1928. He went away on vacation, leaving the bacteria growing in a glass dish in his laboratory. While he was gone, the dish was contaminated with a mold called Penicillium notatum. When Fleming came back, he found that the area around the mold didn't have any bacteria growing on it. That's how the infection-fighting drug penicillin got its start.

■ QUESTIONS TO PONDER ■

1. What bacteria-fighting drug did Alexander Fleming discover accidentally?

2. Who discovered a vaccine for the polio virus?

3. What is a vaccine?

4. Look at the chart again. Which invention do you feel is most important to your daily life? Explain your answer.

Communication Inventions

It is difficult to imagine a time when we were not able to pick up a telephone and speak to someone far away. Even more unimaginable, though, would be a time before paper existed. Several inventions have paved the way for bringing the world closer together.

YEAR	INVENTION	INVENTOR (COUNTRY)
105	paper	Ts'ai Lun (China)
1447	movable type	Johann Gutenberg (Germany)
1795	modern pencil	Nicolas Jacques Conté (France)
1837	telegraph	Samuel F.B. Morse (U.S.)
1845	rotary printing press	Richard M. Hoe (U.S.)
1867	typewriter	Christopher L. Sholes, Carlos Glidden, & Samuel W. Soulé (U.S.)
1870s	telephone	Alexander G. Bell (U.S.); Antonio Meucci (Italy)
1888	ballpoint pen	John Loud (U.S.)
1913	modern radio receiver	Reginald A. Fessenden (U.S.)
1937	xerography copies	Chester Carlson (U.S.)
1942	electronic computer	John V. Atanasoff & Clifford Berry (U.S.)
1944	auto sequence computer	Howard H. Aiken (U.S.)
1955	fiber optics	Narinder S. Kapany (England)
1965	word processor	IBM (U.S.)
1979	cellular telephone	Ericsson Company (Sweden)
1987	laptop computer	Sir Clive Sinclair (England)
1994	digital camera	Apple Computer, Kodak (U.S.)
2002	wind-up cell phone	Motorola (U.S.) & Freeplay Energy Group (England)

Using the word "hello" as a greeting is only as old as the telephone, which was invented in the 1870s. Alexander Graham Bell, the inventor who patented the telephone, suggested that people say "ahoy" when they answered a ring, but this didn't catch on. "Hello" caught on instead. It is related to "hallo," a cry of surprise used in the mid 19th century.

— QUESTIONS TO PONDER —

1. How many years ago was paper invented?

2. In which European country was the original cell phone invented?

3. One of the inventors of the telephone was Alexander G. Bell. What does the "G." in his name stand for?

4. Look at the chart. Are any of the inventions from long ago outdated now because of newer inventions? Give one specific example of an old invention that is no longer used because a newer invention performs the same function faster or better.

Making Life Easier

Without the following inventions, our day-to-day lives would be a little more difficult.

YEAR	INVENTION	INVENTOR (COUNTRY)
1800	electric battery	Alessandro Volta (Italy)
1831	lawn mower	Edwin Budding & John Ferrabee (England)
1834	refrigeration	Jacob Perkins (England)
1846	sewing machine	Elias Howe (U.S.)
1851	cylinder (door) lock	Linus Yale (U.S.)
1879	practical light bulb	Thomas A. Edison (U.S.)
1886	dishwasher	Josephine Cochran (U.S.)
1891	zipper	Whitcomb L. Judson (U.S.)
1901	washing machine	Langmuir Fisher (U.S.)
1903	windshield wipers	Mary Anderson (U.S.)
1907	vacuum cleaner	J. Murray Spangler (U.S.)
1911	air conditioning	Willis H. Carrier (U.S.)
1924	frozen packaged food	Clarence Birdseye (U.S.)
1948	Velcro	Georges de Mestral (Switzerland)
1958	laser	A. L. Schawlow & C. H. Townes (U.S.)
1963	pop-top can	Ermal C. Fraze (U.S.)
1969	cash machine (ATM)	Don Wetzel (U.S.)
1971	food processor	Pierre Verdon (France)
1980	Post-it notes	3M Company (U.S.)

——— QUESTIONS TO PONDER ———

1. In what year was the zipper invented?

2. In what year might you have seen a newspaper headline that read:

   CARPET CLEANING JUST GOT EASIER!

3. When people have to drive their cars on rainy days, they should probably thank this person for her invention.

   a. Josephine Cochran   b. Langmuir Fisher   c. Mary Anderson

4. How many of the inventions above do you use at your school? List the inventions and how they are used.

Entertaining Inventions

Never before have we had as many entertainment options as we do now. It seems that every year a dazzling, new electronic device is invented or improved upon. The list below shows some of the earlier inventions that allowed us to first see things more clearly than we had ever seen and hear things more clearly than we had ever heard—and all in the comfort of our homes!

YEAR	INVENTION	INVENTOR (COUNTRY)
1709	piano	Bartolomeo Cristofori (Italy)
1877	phonograph	Thomas A. Edison (U.S.)
1877	microphone	Emile Berliner (U.S.)
1888	portable camera	George Eastman (U.S.)
1893	moving picture viewer	Thomas A. Edison (U.S.)
1894	motion picture projector	Charles F. Jenkins (U.S.)
1899	tape recorder	Valdemar Poulsen (Denmark)
1923	television*	Vladimir K. Zworykin* (U.S.)
1963	audiocassette	Phillips Corporation (Netherlands)
1963	steel tennis racquet	René Lacoste (France)
1969	videotape cassette	Sony (Japan)
1972	compact disc (CD)	RCA (U.S.)
1972	video game (Pong)	Noland Bushnell (U.S.)
1979	Walkman	Sony (Japan)
1995	DVD (digital video disk)	Matsushita (Japan)

Others who helped invent television include Philo T. Farnsworth (1926) and John Baird (1928).

The MP3 is causing a musical revolution. This format lets you transfer music from your computer or the Web into a portable device. Though these devices can be as small as a watch or pen, they pack about an hour's worth of music. Some new models can even store thousands of songs. More and more, MP3 players are being packaged with other gadgets such as cell phones and cameras. Some MP3 players even include tiny LCD screens. These let you download photo files, and offer video playback. That means you can watch a music video and play your favorite tunes at the same time!

QUESTIONS TO PONDER

1. In what year was the first video game invented?

2. Name the three people who helped invent television.

3. Sony invented the videotape cassette in 1969. How many years later did they invent the Walkman?

4. Which invention listed on this page is most important to your daily life? Do you think your answer will be different in five years? Why or why not?

Top 10 Languages

Would you have guessed that Mandarin, the principal language of China, is the most common spoken language in the world? You may find more surprises in the chart below, which lists languages spoken by at least 100,000,000 native speakers (those for whom the language is their first language, or mother tongue) and some of the places where each one is spoken.

LANGUAGE	WHERE SPOKEN	NATIVE SPEAKERS
Mandarin	China, Taiwan	874,000,000
Hindi	India	366,000,000
English	U.S., Canada, Britain	341,000,000
Spanish	Spain, Latin America	322,000,000
Arabic	Arabian Peninsula	207,000,000
Bengali	India, Bangladesh	207,000,000
Portuguese	Portugal, Brazil	176,000,000
Russian	Russia	167,000,000
Japanese	Japan	125,000,000
German	Germany, Austria	100,000,000

Surprise your friends and family with your knowledge of words from other languages.

ENGLISH	SPANISH	FRENCH	GERMAN	CHINESE
blue	azul	bleu	blau	lan
red	rojo	rouge	rot	hong
green	verde	vert	grun	lu
yellow	amarillo	jaune	gelb	huang
black	negro	noir	schwarz	hei
white	blanco	blanc	weiss	bai
happy !	¡feliz!	bonne	Glückwunsnch	sheng-ri
birthday	¡cumpleaños!	anniversaire!	zum Geburtstag!	kuai le!
hello!	¡hola!	bonjour!	hallo!	ni hao!
good-bye!	¡hasta luego!	au revoir!	auf Wiedersehen	zai-jian!

━━━ QUESTIONS TO PONDER ━━━

1. What is the primary language of India?

     a. Indian   b. Hindi   c. Bengali

2. Which two of the top 10 languages have the same number of native speakers throughout the world?

3. If you were at the Eiffel Tower in Paris, how would you say hello to a native speaker of the country you were visiting?

4. If you could learn one new language, which would it be? Why?

Idioms

Idioms are phrases that mean more than their words put together. If you take them word for word, they might not make much sense! Idioms are a little like puzzles: try imagining a picture or a situation that the phrase suggests, and guess at the meaning from there.

the buck stops here—"taking responsibility for something, instead of blaming someone else." President Harry S. Truman invented this phrase and had a sign made for his desk with those words. Truman liked to play poker, a popular card game. In poker, a marker called a "buck" was placed in front of the player who would be the next to deal the cards. A player who didn't want to deal could pass the buck to the next player.

a flash in the pan—"something that starts out to be a big success but fizzles out quickly." Flintlock muskets had a little pan to be filled with gunpowder. When the trigger was pulled, a spark from the flint would light that powder. It was supposed to burn through a hole in the barrel and light more powder behind the bullet. A "flash in the pan" made light and smoke for a second, but didn't fire the bullet.

footing the bill—"paying." The person who signs his or her name at the bottom, or "foot," of a bill or check (as at a restaurant) is the one who pays. Signing the foot, or "footing it," has come to mean paying.

hat trick—"scoring three times in a game." Used in hockey and soccer, this term came from the English game of cricket. In cricket, a bowler (sort of like a pitcher) tries to knock over three wooden stakes, or wickets, that are guarded by a player with a flat bat. Knocking down three wickets on three straight "pitches" was called a "hat trick." A long time ago, players who did it won a hat.

the jig is up—"the game or trick is exposed." In Shakespeare's time, "jig" was a slang for trick. When the "jig is up," the trick has been discovered.

pull the wool over someone's eyes—"trick or deceive." In the days when gentlemen wore powdered wigs, "wool" was a funny word for hair. Jokesters would knock a man's wig (his wool) down over his eyes so that he couldn't see what was happening.

raining cats and dogs—"raining very heavily." Centuries ago, people thought certain animals had magical powers. Sailors believed cats had something to do with rainstorms. Dogs and wolves were symbols of winds in Norse mythology.

QUESTIONS TO PONDER

1. If a new dance is popular for a short time but then goes out of style, which idiom would you use to describe it?

    a. the jig is up   b. footing the bill   c. a flash in the pan

2. In Norse mythology, what animals were symbols of winds?

3. "The buck stops here" means to take responsibility. What do you think "to pass the buck" means?

4. Have you heard any other idioms that aren't listed here? If not, try to come up with a few of your own. It's okay if they sound silly, as long as there is a reason behind them!

Fun with Words

Here are two ways to have fun with words:

Palindromes

A palindrome is a word, verse, or sentence that reads the same backward and forward. If English were a very old language, the first words ever spoken could have been a palindrome: "Madam, I'm Adam." Or maybe, "Madam in Eden, I'm Adam." The answer Adam got could have been: "Eve." Here are some other palindromes to ponder.

> A warning outside the veterinarian's office could read: **Step on no pets.**
>
> If your aging cats act confused or strange, you may be dealing with **senile felines.**
>
> Have you ever asked yourself: **Do geese see God?**
>
> After trying unsuccessfully to lift a heavy rock, you might shout: **O, stone, be not so!**
>
> You're making a drawing of your family, but you're not sure you have it right, so you could ask your brother: **Did I draw Della too tall, Edward? I did?**

Anagrams

An anagram takes all the letters of a word or phrase and switches them around in a way that still make sense. The best ones are funny, or surprising in some way. For example, one anagram for "school day" is "shady cool."

Easy ones:

glare	thicken
LARGE	KITCHEN

Here's a really tough one:
The World Almanac for Kids

KIDS CALL EARTHWORM NO FAD ARMADILLO FETCH DARK SNOW

Harder:

lunch break	cheerleader
A BENCH LURK	DECLARE HERE
elementary school	middle school
A MOST LONELY CHEER	SOME OLD CHILD

QUESTIONS TO PONDER

1. Which of the following words is a palindrome?

   a. puppy   b. Adam   c. level

2. Try to create a palindrome of your own. Make it at least two words long.

3. Can you unscramble this anagram to come up with the name of a famous golfer: DOES IT GROW?

4. Create an anagram of your own. You can use a person's name or an object . . . or just about anything.

Word History

The English language is always changing. New words become part of the vocabulary all the time. Others become outdated and aren't used much anymore. Either way, when you open your mouth, you have thousands and thousands of words to choose from. Where did all these words come from? Sometimes new words are named after people.

How would you like to have your name added as a word to the English language? A few people have been so lucky . . . or unlucky. An **eponym** is a word that comes from a person's name. Here are a few:

boycott: In 1880 a man in Ireland named Charles Boycott refused to lower rents. As a result, the public refused to have anything to do with him. The term **boycott** now means to avoid a person, organization, or company, or refuse to buy certain products, as a protest.

 **cardigan:** The 7th earl of Cardigan (in Wales) had the soldiers in his military regiment wear knitted sweaters or jackets that fastened up the front. People then began to call this type of sweater a **cardigan.**

leotard: Julius Leotard was a French aerial gymnast who lived during the 19th century. His name became attached to the tight-fitting garment he wore when he performed.

 sandwich: John Montagu, the 4th earl of Sandwich (in England), wanted something he could eat without having to get up from the table where he played games. The tasty, easy-to-hold **sandwich** fit the bill.

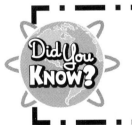 **Did You Know?**

SOCCER *got its name in an odd way. In London in the 1860s, several clubs formed a group in order to agree to the same rules for football. Those who wanted to allow the ball to be carried left the group and started "rugby." The game played by the remaining clubs was called "Association Football," then "socca" for short, and later "soccer."*

QUESTIONS TO PONDER

1. What sport was invented by former soccer players who wanted to be allowed to carry the ball during games?

2. In what country was the sandwich invented?

3. Which two eponyms are words that describe clothing?

4. Can you create an eponym of your own? Use the name of a celebrity or historical figure to create an eponym that makes sense.

History of Money

Why Did People Start Using Money?

Do you know how money came to be? At first, people bartered, which means they traded goods they had for things they needed. A farmer who had cattle might want to have salt to preserve meat, or cloth to make clothing. For this farmer, a cow became a "medium of exchange"—a way of getting things the farmer did not make or grow. Cattle became a form of money. Whatever people agreed to use for trade became the earliest kinds of money.

Throughout history, the following objects have been used as money:
- ► *knives, rice, and spades in China around 3000 B.C.*
- ► *cattle and clay tablets in Babylonia around 2500 B.C.*
- ► *wampum (beads) and beaver fur by Native Americans of the Northeast around A.D. 1500*
- ► *tobacco by early American colonists around 1650*
- ► *whales' teeth by the Pacific peoples on the island of Fiji, until the early 1900s*

Why Did Governments Start Issuing Money?

Governments were interested in issuing money because the money itself had value. If a government could gain control over the manufacture of money, it could increase its own wealth—often simply by making more money.

The first government to make coins that looked alike and use them as money is thought to be the Greek city-state of Lydia in the 7th century B.C. These Lydian coins were actually bean-shaped lumps made from a mixture of gold and silver.

By the Middle Ages (about A.D. 800–1100), gold had become a popular medium for trade in Europe. But gold was heavy and difficult to carry, and the cities and the roads of Europe at that time were dangerous places to carry large amounts of gold. So merchants and goldsmiths began issuing notes promising to pay gold to the person carrying the note. These "promissory notes" were the beginning of paper money in Europe. In the early 1700s, France's government became the first in Europe to issue paper money that looked alike. Paper money was probably also invented in China, where the explorer Marco Polo saw it in the 1280s.

QUESTIONS TO PONDER

1. What is a synonym for the word barter?
   - a. buy   b. sell   c. trade

2. Which of the following is not mentioned on this page as having been used as money?
   - a. tobacco   b. beans   c. rice

3. Why did governments make the change from golden money to paper money?

4. Name each of the coins in your country's currency. Now name each historical figure whose face is on each of those coins.

The Euro

Citizens of 12 countries in Europe (see below) were excited about the crisp new paper money and sparkling new coins they had starting in January 2002. This new currency, called the euro, is good in all 12 countries. Switching to the euro was a big job. In a short time, banks had to get money worth 600 billion euros into the hands of 300 million people.

Many Germans were sad to see their marks disappear. People in France and Italy miss their francs and lire. But now money will flow easily from one country to another. This should make it easier to complete big financial deals between countries. And think how easy it will be for tourists. They can use the same kind of money to pay for a slice of pizza whether it's in Italy or in Belgium. Americans in Europe can easily figure what something costs because the euro and U.S. dollar are worth about the same—the euro equaled about $1.07 in U.S. money in the spring of 2003.

Some things didn't change. Criminals wasted no time pulling off the first euro theft. On January 1, two men robbed a bank in Spain of 90,000 euros.

Countries in the European Union

Switched to Euro		Still Use Their Own Currencies
Austria	Ireland	Denmark
Belgium	Italy	Great Britain
Finland	Luxembourg	Sweden
France	The Netherlands	
Germany	Portugal	
Greece	Spain	

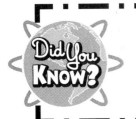

► *The science and study of coins is called **numismatics**. When you look at old coins, you can learn about a nation's history—its kings, queens, war heroes, famous buildings, and symbols of power and authority, such as shields or coats of arms.*

QUESTIONS TO PONDER

1. Which of the following countries does not use the euro as its currency?

    a. Sweden   b. Luxembourg   c. Germany

2. What is the science and study of coins called?

3. What percentage of countries in the European Union use the euro as their currency? (*Hint:* Twelve out of fifteen countries in the European Union use the euro.)

4. Do you think it is a good idea for most of Europe to use the same currency? Why do you think three of the countries decided not to use the euro?

What Do You Want to Be?

More than 130 million people in the United States have jobs. You see many of them every day—teachers, bus drivers, or cashiers. Many jobs exist that you may not have ever heard of or thought of: aerospace engineer or actuary, for example. Although new jobs are constantly created, some jobs become unnecessary as different ways are found to do the work.

Here are just a few of the jobs people have today. Do you think any of them will interest you when you're ready to start your career?

COLLEGE PROFESSORS

College teachers, who are called professors, usually have a Ph.D., or a doctoral degree, in the subject they teach. That means they took courses and did special research for several years after graduating from college. Professors teach students and grade papers and tests. They also do research and write about the subject they teach.

NURSES

Caring for patients and helping doctors are two of the most important responsibilities nurses have. People are living longer and scientists are finding new ways to treat and cure diseases, so nurses are needed more and more.

COMPUTER TECHNICIANS

As more and more people own or use computers, more workers are needed to repair the machines. Computer technicians also install and replace computer equipment.

FIREFIGHTERS

Fires can occur anywhere, such as in a city building or in a forest. A firefighter's most important job is to rescue people. Saving homes and other property from destruction is also important. Firefighters often use large trucks, tall ladders, and other heavy equipment. They have a dangerous job, and people regard them as heroes.

QUESTIONS TO PONDER

1. What is another name for a college teacher?

    a. Ph.D.   b. professor   c. actuary

2. Why are nurses needed more and more these days?

3. Of the four jobs listed in boxes on this page, which one would not have existed 100 years ago?

4. Which of the jobs listed on this page would you be most interested in doing? Which would you be least interested in? Explain your answers.

Making a Budget

A budget is a plan that estimates how much money a person, a business, or a government will receive during a period of time, how much money will be spent and what it will be spent on, and how much money will be left over (if any).

A BALANCED BUDGET

A budget is **balanced** when the amount of money you receive equals the amount of money you spend. A budget is **in deficit** when the amount of money you spend is greater than the amount of money you have.

FAMILY BUDGET

Do you know what your family spends money on? Do you know where your family's income comes from? The chart below shows some sources of income and typical yearly expenses for a family's budget.

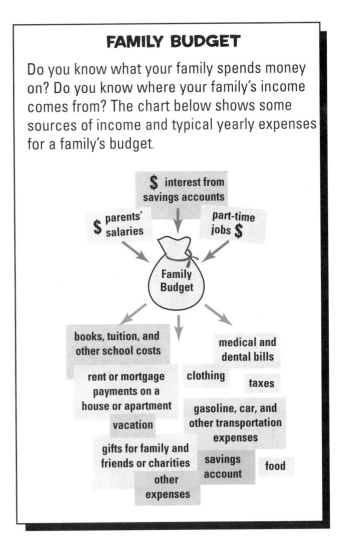

QUESTIONS TO PONDER

1. *Complete this sentence:* When the amount of money you spend equals the amount of money you receive, your budget is _____.

2. *Complete this sentence:* When the amount of money you spend is more than the amount of money you receive, your budget is _____.

3. Look at the Family Budget chart. The chart shows 11 things that the family's money is being spent on. Rank those things from 1–11, with 1 being the most important expense and 11 being the least important expense in your opinion.

4. How well do you think you will be able to manage your budget when you get your first job? What are some things that you know you will want to buy?

Afghanistan

Afghanistan, a country on the continent of Asia, has a long, difficult history of war and political unrest. Under the Taliban, the Muslim fundamentalist group that ruled Afghanistan for six years, there were many strict rules. For example, girls were not allowed to go to school. When the Taliban was overthrown in 2001, life remained hard. Many families still live in crowded mud houses, with no heat in winter and not enough food. Many kids still can't go to school because they have to do chores like getting water or taking care of farm animals. But they still find time to have fun. They play games like hide and seek and *topay-danda*, a kind of stickball. Kite flying was forbidden under the Taliban but has become popular again.

More information on Afghanistan

Capital	Kabul
Location of Nation	Southern Asia
Neighbors	Iran, Pakistan, Tajikistan, Turkmenistan, Uzbekistan
Area	250,000 sq. mi. (647,500 sq. km.)
Population	27,755,775
Language	Afghan Persian, Pashtu

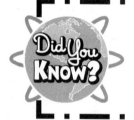

Millions of landmines, buried during decades of war, litter the Afghan countryside. In 1997 over 120 countries signed a treaty to ban the use of landmines and to remove pre-existing ones.

QUESTIONS TO PONDER

1. What Muslim fundamentalist group ruled Afghanistan at the end of the 20th century?

2. How many countries border Afghanistan?

3. In Afghanistan, children play a game called topay-danda. Which American game is *most similar* to topay-danda?

    a. baseball   b. football   c. basketball

4. How many countries border the country in which you live? Do you think it is an advantage or a disadvantage for a country to have many neighbors nearby?

Canada

Canada is a large country that occupies most of the northern part of North America. The first people in Canada were the Micmac Indians and the Inuit, or Eskimos, who came to Canada from Asia thousands of years ago. In fact, many native people still live there today.

In the 1600s, Canada was settled by English and French fur traders. Today, it is a bilingual country. English and French are both official languages, and many Canadians can speak both languages.

Canada is bigger than the United States but has only one-ninth as many people. Three out of four people live in urban areas, but there is plenty of open space.

Most of the land is covered in snow all winter. Ice hockey, skiing, and curling are popular sports.

Fast Facts About Canada

Capital	Area	Population	Currency	Language(s)
Ottawa	3,851,810 sq. miles (9,976,140 sq. km)	31,902,268	$1 = 1.5 Canadian dollars	English French

The Canada/U.S. boundary is the world's longest undefended border. This means that citizens of each country are free to pass back and forth between the two countries.

▬▬▬ QUESTIONS TO PONDER ▬▬▬

1. What is another name for an Eskimo?

2. What does the word bilingual mean?

3. If you had 15 Canadian dollars, about how much money would you have in American dollars?

4. What are some advantages to having an undefended border between countries? What are some disadvantages?

The United Nations

The United Nations (UN) was started in 1945 after World War II. The first members of the UN were 50 nations that met in San Francisco, California. They signed an agreement known as the UN Charter. By early 2002, the UN had 189 independent countries as members—not counting East Timor, which was moving close to independence, and Switzerland, which in 2002 finally voted to seek membership.

The UN Charter lists these purposes:

1. to keep worldwide peace and security
2. to develop friendly relations among countries
3. to help countries cooperate in solving problems ·
4. to promote respect for human rights and basic freedoms
5. to be a center that helps countries achieve their goals

FAST FACTS ABOUT THE UNITED NATIONS

► The UN has its own fire department, security force, and postal service. Its UN post office sells stamps that can be used only to send mail from the UN.

► The flags of all member nations fly in front of UN headquarters. They are in alphabetical order, from Afghanistan to Zimbabwe.

► The secretary-general (chief officer) of the UN is Kofi Annan of Ghana. In June 2001 the General Assembly unanimously reelected him to a second five-year term.

► The United Nations and Kofi Annan shared the Nobel Peace Prize in 2001. It wasn't the first time for the UN. The UN Peacekeeping Forces won it in 1988, and the UN High Commissioner for Refugees won in 1954 and 1981. UNICEF (United Nations Children's Fund) won it in 1965, and the International Labor Organization, a special agency associated with the UN, received it in 1969.

In 1945, John D. Rockefeller Jr., drawing from the Rockefeller family fortune, bought a six-block site along New York City's East River for $8.5 million, and donated it to the UN for its headquarters. He also built Rockefeller Center in New York and gave most of the money to create Colonial Williamsburg in Virginia.

——— QUESTIONS TO PONDER ———

1. Who was the secretary-general of the UN when terrorists attacked the United States on September 11, 2001?

2. In which city is the United Nations' headquarters located?

3. List the dates of the United Nations' Nobel Peace Prizes in chronological order.

4. How important do you think it is for nations of the world to work together? Give specific examples to support your answer.

The United Nations *(cont.)*

Here's a look at how the UN is organized:

GENERAL ASSEMBLY

What It Does: discusses world problems, admits new members, appoints the secretary-general, decides the UN budget

Members: All members of the UN belong to the General Assembly; each country has one vote.

SECURITY COUNCIL

What It Does: discusses questions of peace and security.

Members: Five permanent members (China, France, Great Britain, Russia, and the United States), and 10 members elected by the General Assembly for two-year terms.

ECONOMIC AND SOCIAL COUNCIL

What It Does: deals with issues related to trade, economic development, industry, population, children, food, education, health, and human rights.

Members: Fifty-four member countries elected for three-year terms.

INTERNATIONAL COURT OF JUSTICE (WORLD COURT) located at The Hague, Netherlands

What It Does: highest court for disputes between countries.

Members: Fifteen judges, each from a different country, elected to nine-year terms.

SECRETARIAT

What It Does: carries out day-to-day operations of the UN.

Members: UN staff, headed by the secretary-general.

In May 2002, some 3,000 delegates, including more than 250 kids, from over 180 nations met at the UN for a special Children's Summit. They reviewed progress made in dealing with children's needs around the world.

═══ QUESTIONS TO PONDER ═══

1. In what country is the UN World Court located?

2. At any given time, how many nations are members of the UN Security Council?

3. Which of the following areas would be dealt with by the UN Economic and Social Council?

   a. war   b. UN budget   c. famine

4. Would you like to have been a member of the UN Children's Summit? If you would have been allowed to speak to the UN members about one issue facing children today, what issue would you have discussed?

Finding the Area

OF A SQUARE:

A square is a plane figure with four equal sides, like the figure you see here. To find the area for a square, use this formula: **side x side** (**side x side** can also be written as **S²**, pronounced "side squared").

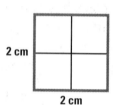

2 cm

2 cm

Each side of this square is 2 centimeters long. So the area is 2 x 2, or 4. These are no longer centimeters but **square centimeters**, like the smaller squares inside the big one.

OF A TRIANGLE:

A triangle is a three-sided plane figure. The prefix "tri" means three, which refers to the three points where the sides of a triangle meet.

To find the area for a triangle use **½ x (base x height)** (first multiply the base by the height, then multiply that number by ½).

This triangle has a base of 2 centimeters and a height of 3 centimeters. So the area will be 3 square centimeters.

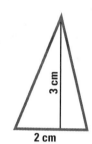

3 cm

2 cm

OF A CIRCLE:

The distance around a circle is called its **circumference**. All the points on the circumference are an equal distance from the center. That distance from center to circumference is called the **radius**. A **diameter** is any straight line that has both ends on the circle and passes through its center. It's twice as long as the radius.

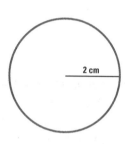

2 cm

To find the area for a circle you need to use π—a number called pi that is always the same, about 3.14. The formula for area is: **π x radius x radius** (or **π x radius squared**).

For instance, this circle has a radius of 2 centimeters, so its area = π x 2 x 2, or π x 2²; that is, 3.14 x 4. This equals 12.56 square centimeters.

In math, π, the Greek letter for pi, stands for the number you get when you divide the circumference of a circle by its diameter. This number is always the same (about 3.14), no matter how big the circle is! The Babylonians discovered this over 4,000 years ago.

Yes, π is about 3.14, but no one can give its exact value. It doesn't divide exactly, and so the number goes on forever. In 1999 a super computer figured out the value to over 200 billion places to the right of the decimal point. As for humans, a Japanese man established a record in 1995 by being able to memorize and recite π to over 42,000 places to the right of the decimal point!

QUESTIONS TO PONDER

1. What is the distance around a circle called?
2. What is the area of a square in which one of the sides is 6 cm long?
   a. 36 cm   b. 12 sq. cm   c. 36 sq. cm
3. Many countries have flags that are tricolor. How many colors do tricolor flags have?
4. Most people would not be able to understand why someone would want to memorize a number over 42,000 digits long. Do you have any hobbies that are very important to you but that other people might not view as "important"?

Numerals in Ancient Civilization

People have been counting since the earliest of times. This is what some numerals looked like in different cultures:

MODERN	1	2	3	4	5	6	7	8	9	10	20	50	100
Egyptian	I	II	III	IIII	IIII	IIII	IIII	IIII	IIII	∩	∩∩	∩∩∩∩∩	ϑ
Babylonian													
Greek	A	B	Γ	Δ	E	F	Z	H	θ	I	K	N	P
Mayan													
Chinese	一	二	三	四	五	六	七	八	九	十	二十	五十	百
Hindu	I	੨	੩	੪	੫	੬	੭	੮	੯	10	੨0	੪0	100
Arabic	I	٢	٣	٤	٥	٦	٧	٨	٩	١٥	٢٥	٨٥	١٥٥

ROMAN NUMERALS

Roman numerals are still used today. The symbols used for different numbers are the letters I (1), V (5), X (10), L (50), C (100), D (500), and M (1,000). If one Roman numeral is followed by a larger one, the first is subtracted from the second. For example, IV means 5 – 1 = 4. Think of it as "one less than five." On the other hand, if one Roman numeral is followed by another that is equal or smaller, add them together. Thus, XII means 10 + 1 + 1 = 12. Can you put the year you were born in Roman numerals?

1	I	14	XIV	90	XC
2	II	15	XV	100	C
3	III	16	XVI	200	CC
4	IV	17	XVII	300	CCC
5	V	18	XVIII	400	CD
6	VI	19	XIX	500	D
7	VII	20	XX	600	DC
8	VIII	30	XXX	700	DCC
9	IX	40	XL	800	DCCC
10	X	50	L	900	CM
11	XI	60	LX	1,000	M
12	XII	70	LXX	2,000	MM
13	XIII	80	LXXX	3,000	MMM

QUESTIONS TO PONDER

1. What is the Greek symbol for the number 8?

2. How old are you? Write your age in Egyptian numerals.

3. The Roman empire fell in A.D. 476. What is 476 in Roman numerals?

    a. CDLXXVI   b. XXIVD   c. CCCCLXXVI

4. Look at the Egyptian, Babylonian, Mayan, and Roman numerals. Of these four systems of counting, which one do you think would be the easiest to learn and use? Which would be the most difficult? Explain your answers.

Planes and Solids

When a figure is flat (two-dimensional), it is a plane figure. When a figure takes up space (three-dimensional), it is a solid figure. The flat surface of a solid figure is called a face. Plane and solid figures come in many shapes.

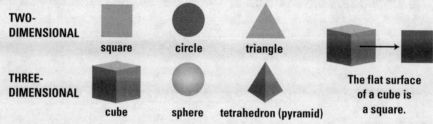

TWO-DIMENSIONAL: square, circle, triangle

THREE-DIMENSIONAL: cube, sphere, tetrahedron (pyramid)

The flat surface of a cube is a square.

WHAT ARE POLYGONS?

A polygon is a two-dimensional figure with three or more straight sides. A square is a polygon. Polygons have different numbers of sides—and each has a different name. If the sides are all the same length and all the angles between the sides are equal, the polygon is called regular. If the sides are of different lengths or the angles are not equal, the polygon is called irregular. At right are some regular and irregular polygons.

NAME & NUMBER OF SIDES	REGULAR	IRREGULAR
TRIANGLE – 3		
QUADRILATERAL OR TETRAGON – 4		
PENTAGON – 5		
HEXAGON – 6		
HEPTAGON – 7		
OCTAGON – 8		
NONAGON – 9		
DECAGON – 10		

WHAT ARE POLYHEDRONS?

A polyhedron is a three-dimensional figure with four or more faces. Each face on a polyhedron is a polygon. Below are some polyhedrons with many faces.

tetrahedron 4 faces	hexahedron 6 faces	octahedron 8 faces	dodecahedron 12 faces	icosahedron 20 faces

QUESTIONS TO PONDER

1. What do you call a six-sided two-dimensional object?
   a. hexahedron   b. hexagon   c. cube

2. Look at this figure: ⬠ . Which of the following would best describe it?
   a. solid figure   b. irregular octahedron   c. irregular octagon

3. What percentage of the faces of a tetrahedron are triangles?

4. How many different polygons and polyhedrons can you find in your classroom? Make a list.

Number Prefixes

Did you know that you can sometimes help determine the meaning of a word by looking at its first few letters? There are some groups of letters—called prefixes—that are used to begin words, and these prefixes give you a clue about the meaning of the word.

Look at the chart below. After each number are one or more prefixes used to form words that include that number. Knowing what the prefix stands for can help you understand the meaning of the word. For example, a monorail has one track. A pentagon has five sides. And an octopus has eight tentacles (or arms).

1/2	semi-	semicircle, semiannual
1	uni-, mon-, mono-	unicycle, unicorn, monarch, monorail
2	bi-	bicycle, binary, binoculars, bifocals
3	tri-	tricycle, triangle, trilogy, trio
4	quadr-, tetr-	quadrangle, quadruplet, tetrahedron
5	pent-, quint-	pentagon, pentathlon, quintuplet
6	hex-, sext-	hexagon, sextuplet, sextet
7	hept-, sept-	heptathlon, septuplet
8	oct-	octave, octet, octopus, octagon
9	non-	nonagon, nonet
10	dec-	decade, decibel, decimal
100	cent-	centipede, century
1000	kilo-	kilogram, kilometer, kilowatt
million	mega-	megabyte, megahertz
billion	giga-	gigabyte, gigawatt

September gets its name from the calendar used in Roman times, when it was the seventh month (the Roman year began in March). Similarly, October was so named because it used to be the eighth month of the year.

QUESTIONS TO PONDER

1. If a mother just gave birth to quintuplets, how many children did she just give birth to?

2. If a country is celebrating its centennial anniversary, for how many years has it been a country?

3. If you were given a semi-monthly allowance of $1, how much money would you make in one year?

4. Invent a new object or animal and give it a name that contains a number prefix. Just as a unicorn has one horn and a bicycle has two wheels, your object or animal's name should help describe it.

Everyday Science

Every day, things happen all around you that might seem mysterious. But most of them can be explained scientifically. Here are just a few questions you might ask yourself when you observe the world around you:

Why Is the Sky Blue?

Sunlight makes the sky blue. Light from the Sun is actually white until it reaches Earth's atmosphere. Then it hits water vapor, dust, and other particles in the air and scatters in different directions. White light is made up of all the colors of the spectrum. Since blue is scattered much more than any other color, blue is what we see when we look up at a clear sky. During sunrises and sunsets, we see red and orange because the sun is closer to the horizon, scattering blue light out of our line of sight.

Why Do Leaves Change Color in the Fall?

Tree leaves contain a chemical called **chlorophyll**, which makes them look green in spring and summer. Chlorophyll helps capture light energy from the sun and change it to a chemical form, like sugar, as food for the tree. The leaves also contain yellow and orange carotenoids (the substance that makes carrots orange), but the green chlorophyll in spring and summer masks those other colors. In the fall, as days get shorter and colder, the chlorophyll breaks down and the yellow and orange show up. If the temperature falls below 45 degrees at night, sugar made during the day gets trapped in the leaves. This is what makes sugar maple leaves look red.

What Causes Rainbows?

The light we usually see (visible light) is made up of different frequencies, or colors, in a certain range, called the **spectrum**. The colors of the visible spectrum are red, orange, yellow, green, blue, indigo, and violet. White light is a mixture of all these colors. A prism can separate the frequencies mixed in a beam of white light. When you see a rainbow, the tiny water droplets in the air act as many tiny prisms, separating the sun's white light into the colors of the spectrum.

What Causes Thunder?

Lightning does. In an instant, a bolt of lightning can heat the air around it up to 60,000°F. The heated air expands violently, like an explosion. As the air expands it also cools quickly and starts to contract. This quick expansion and contraction of air creates the shock waves we hear as thunder.

Think of popping a balloon. When you blow it up, you are putting the air under pressure. Why? Because air molecules in the balloon are packed more tightly than they are in the air around it. The rubber keeps the air inside the balloon from spreading out. When the balloon breaks, the air expands rapidly (like the air superheated by lightning). The molecules from inside the balloon push against those on the outside—creating a shock wave that you hear as a "pop."

QUESTIONS TO PONDER

1. What color is the light from the sun?

   a. yellow   b. blue   c. white

2. What chemical makes tree leaves look green in the spring and summer?

3. What might you create when playing with a hose on a sunny day?

   a. blue sky   b. thunder   c. rainbow

4. What natural everyday occurrence do you find most mysterious? Choose one that isn't explained on this page. What do you think causes it?

DNA

Every cell in every living thing (or organism) has DNA, a molecule that contains all the information about that organism. Lengths of connected DNA molecules, called genes, are like tiny pieces of a secret code. They determine what each organism is like in great detail.

Genes are passed on from parents to children, and no two organisms (except identical twins) have the same DNA. Many things about us—the color of our eyes or hair, whether we're tall or short, the size of our feet—depend on the genes we inherited from our parents.

WHAT MAKES US HUMAN

The human genome is the DNA code for our species. In 2000, the U.S. Human Genome Project reached a milestone: it identified the 3.1 billion separate codes in human DNA. In 2001, researchers reported that the human genome contains about 30,000 to 40,000 genes. For the first time, we got an outline of the genetic code for the human race.

Surprisingly, humans don't have that many more genes than the roundworm, which has about 20,000! But we do have three times as many kinds of proteins as the fly or worm because of a process in humans called "alternative splicing." This means that the same gene can produce more than one kind of protein. By studying genes, scientists can learn more about hereditary diseases and get a better idea of how human beings evolved.

A clone is an organism that has developed from a cell of just one other organism. This means it has the exact same DNA as its parent. Scientists have been able to clone mammals artificially. The most famous clone was a sheep named Dolly, born in Scotland in 1996. Dolly developed arthritis sooner than most sheep do. Scientists don't know whether this was because she was cloned or for some other reason. But labs that have cloned cattle, sheep, and goats say the animals that survive to adulthood are normal in every way they can measure.

In February 2002, researchers in Texas announced the birth of "CC" (carbon copy), the world's first cloned cat. CC has exactly the same DNA as Rainbow, the cat she was cloned from. But these two cats look different. This is because calico patterns on cats are caused by random changes during their growth in the womb, rather than by genes.

Human cloning may also be possible one day. But many people believe human cloning would be wrong.

QUESTIONS TO PONDER

1. What is the name given to lengths of connected DNA molecules?
    - a. splices
    - b. clones
    - c. genes

2. About how many more genes does a human genome contain than a roundworm?

3. Why do identical twins look identical?

4. Do you think that cloning humans should be legal? Why or why not?

The Elements

Everything we see and use is made up of basic ingredients called elements. There are more than 100 elements. Most have been found in nature. Some are created by scientists in labs.

Elements Found in Earth's Crust
(percent by weight)

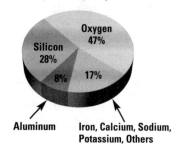

Oxygen 47%
Silicon 28%
8%
17%
Aluminum
Iron, Calcium, Sodium, Potassium, Others

Elements Found in the Atmosphere
(percent by volume)

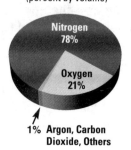

Nitrogen 78%
Oxygen 21%
1% Argon, Carbon Dioxide, Others

IT ALL STARTS WITH AN ATOM

The smallest possible piece of an element that has all the properties of the original element is called an **atom**. Each tiny atom is made up of even smaller particles called **protons, neutrons,** and **electrons.** These are made up of even smaller particles called **quarks**.

To tell one element from another, scientists count the number of protons in an atom. The total number of protons is called the element's **atomic number**. All of the atoms of an element have the same number of protons and electrons, but some atoms have a different number of neutrons. For example, carbon-12 has six protons and six neutrons, and carbon-13 has six protons and seven neutrons.

We call the amount of matter in an atom its atomic mass. Carbon-13 has a greater atomic mass than carbon-12. The average atomic mass of all of the different atoms of the same element is called the element's **atomic weight**. Every element has a different atomic number and a different atomic weight.

When scientists write the names of elements, they often use a symbol instead of spelling out the full name. The symbol for each element is one or two letters. Scientists write O for oxygen and He for helium. The symbols usually come from the English name for the element (C for carbon). Some, however, come from the element's Latin name. For example, the symbol for gold is Au, which is short for Aurum, the Latin word for gold.

——— QUESTIONS TO PONDER ———

1. What is the most common element found in Earth's atmosphere?

2. Which of the following are the smallest?

    a. protons   b. neutrons   c. quarks

3. What type of graph is used on this page to show the elements found in Earth's crust?

    a. bar grap   b. pie chart   c. line graph

4. H_2O is the chemical symbol for water. What other chemical symbols do you know? How could you find out more chemical symbols?

Some Famous Scientists

Over time, many great scientists have helped explain and improve the world in which we live. Here are a few of those men and women and the contributions they made in the field of science.

Science Timeline

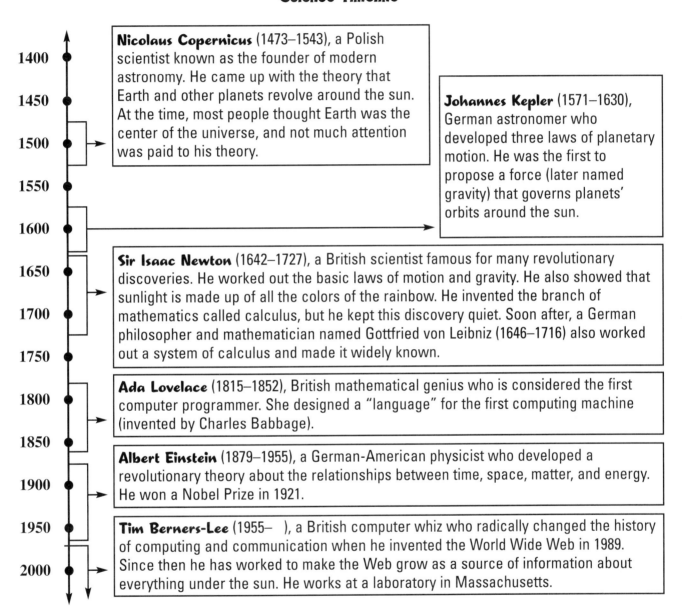

Nicolaus Copernicus (1473–1543), a Polish scientist known as the founder of modern astronomy. He came up with the theory that Earth and other planets revolve around the sun. At the time, most people thought Earth was the center of the universe, and not much attention was paid to his theory.

Johannes Kepler (1571–1630), German astronomer who developed three laws of planetary motion. He was the first to propose a force (later named gravity) that governs planets' orbits around the sun.

Sir Isaac Newton (1642–1727), a British scientist famous for many revolutionary discoveries. He worked out the basic laws of motion and gravity. He also showed that sunlight is made up of all the colors of the rainbow. He invented the branch of mathematics called calculus, but he kept this discovery quiet. Soon after, a German philosopher and mathematician named Gottfried von Leibniz (1646–1716) also worked out a system of calculus and made it widely known.

Ada Lovelace (1815–1852), British mathematical genius who is considered the first computer programmer. She designed a "language" for the first computing machine (invented by Charles Babbage).

Albert Einstein (1879–1955), a German-American physicist who developed a revolutionary theory about the relationships between time, space, matter, and energy. He won a Nobel Prize in 1921.

Tim Berners-Lee (1955–   ), a British computer whiz who radically changed the history of computing and communication when he invented the World Wide Web in 1989. Since then he has worked to make the Web grow as a source of information about everything under the sun. He works at a laboratory in Massachusetts.

QUESTIONS TO PONDER

1. Which of the above scientists has been awarded a Nobel Prize?

2. Who worked out a system of calculus and made it widely known?

3. Of the following pairs of scientists, which pairs' works were most closely related?

    a. Lovelace & Berners-Lee   b. Berners-Lee & Einstein   c. Newton & Lovelace

4. Which of the discoveries or inventions of the scientists on this page most affects your daily life? Give specific reasons for your choice.

Braille

Many blind people read with their fingers, using a system of raised dots called Braille. Braille was developed by Louis Braille (1809–1852) in France in 1826, when he was still a teenager.

The Braille alphabet, numbers, punctuation, and speech sounds are shown by 63 different combinations of six raised dots arranged in a grid like this:

All the letters in the basic Braille alphabet are lowercase. Special symbols are added to show that what follows is a capital letter or a number. The white circles on the grid below show the raised dots.

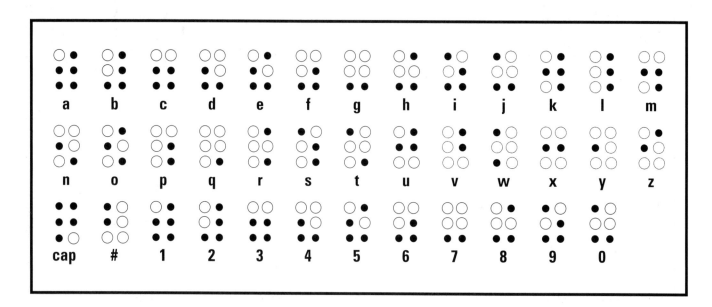

QUESTIONS TO PONDER

1. In which country and on which continent was Braille developed?

2. What color is spelled out here?

3. What color is spelled out here?

4. How has the invention of Braille helped people who are blind? What other advancements or inventions have been made to help people with other disabilities?

Sign Language

Many people who are deaf or hearing-impaired, and cannot hear spoken words, talk with their fingers instead of their voices. To do this, they use a system of manual signs (the manual alphabet), or finger spelling, in which the fingers are used to form letters and words. Originally developed in France by Abbe Charles Michel De l'Epee in the late 1700s, the manual alphabet was later brought to the United States by Laurent Clerc (1785–1869), a Frenchman who taught people who were deaf.

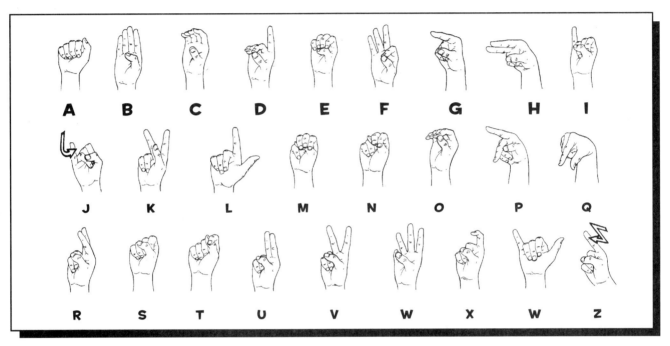

© National Association of the Deaf

QUESTIONS TO PONDER

1. Who brought sign language to the United States?

2. What does the word *manual* mean?

    a. automatic   b. done by hands   c. loud

3. What animal is being signed here?

4. Practice signing the letters of your name and other simple words. Try signing to a friend to see if they can understand what you are "saying." In what other ways do humans communicate with body gestures?

Road Signs

Signs and symbols give us information at a glance. In the days when most people could not read, pictures helped them find their way around. Today, many of the same symbols are used the world over.

Look at the following road signs. Many of them alert drivers to dangers that may lie ahead.

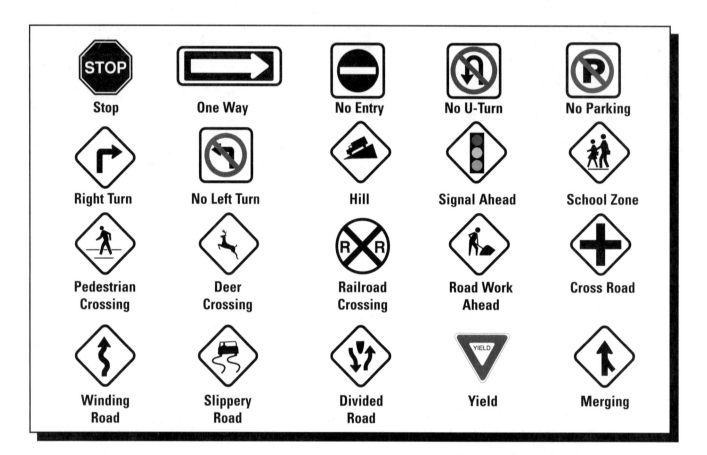

QUESTIONS TO PONDER

1. Which of the following signs would you expect to see if you were driving along a steep mountain road?

   a.   b.   c.

2. Which of the following signs would you expect to see if you were coming up to a crosswalk?

   a.   b.   c.

3. Why do you think road signs feature symbols instead of words?

4. On the back of this page, create a new sign that tells drivers that talking on their cell phones while driving is not allowed.

Code Talkers

In 1918, during the final days of World War I, an American Army captain overheard two soldiers speaking in their native Choctaw language. He didn't understand the words, but he understood something more important. The Germans, who had broken all the U.S. radio codes used so far, would be just as puzzled by Choctaw as he was. The captain's idea led to a secret program of the U.S. military. In World War II, Navajo Indian "code talkers" used a coded form of their language to send secret U.S. military messages in the Pacific. The Japanese could not understand this double code. Comanche soldiers in Europe talked right past the Germans, and other tribes also used their languages as codes, too. When there were no Native American words for a military term or the name of a country, the code talkers used other words instead.

This chart shows a few examples:

Military Term	Native American Substitute
tanks	turtle
battleship	whale
fighter plane	hummingbird
bomber	buzzard

In 2001, 29 Navajo code talkers were awarded the Congressional Gold Medal. President George W. Bush personally presented the medals to four of the five code talkers still living.

turtle

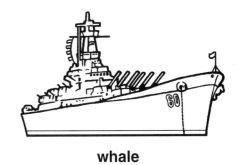

whale

———— QUESTIONS TO PONDER ————

1. In which war were Navajo Indian code talkers used by the U.S. military?

2. When speaking in code, what did Comanches call tanks?

3. Why do you think the Navajo code talkers chose the native word for "buzzard" to represent bomber planes?

4. Imagine that you are a code talker. Come up with a code word for each of these words:

   - computer
   - cell phone
   - TV set

Our Solar System

Nine planets, including Earth, travel around the sun. These planets, together with the sun, make up our solar system.

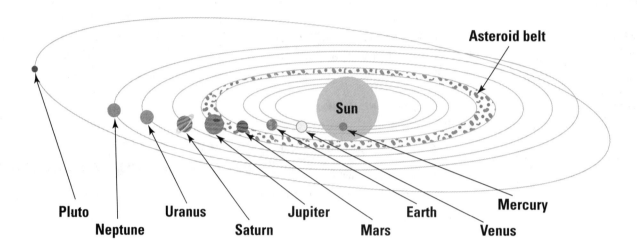

The planets move around the sun along oval-shaped paths called **orbits**. One complete path around the sun is called a **revolution**. Earth takes one year, or 365¼ days, to make one revolution around the sun. Planets that are farther away from the sun take longer. Some planets have one or more moons. A moon orbits a planet in much the same way that the planets orbit the sun.

Each planet also spins (or rotates) on its **axis**. An axis is an imaginary line running through the center of a planet. The time it takes Earth to rotate on its axis equals one day.

Did you know that the sun is a star, like the other stars you see at night? It is a typical, medium-size star. But because the sun is much closer to our planet than any other star, we can study it in great detail. The diameter of the sun is 864,000 miles—more than 100 times Earth's diameter. The gravity of the sun is nearly 28 times the gravity of Earth.

━━ QUESTIONS TO PONDER ━━

1. The paths along which a planet moves around the sun is called _____.

     a. an orbit   b. a revolution   c. an axis

2. There is an asteroid belt between which two planets?

     a. Mercury and Venus   b. Jupiter and Saturn   c. Mars and Jupiter

3. Look at the diagram on this page. Which planet seems to have an orbit around the sun that is shaped differently than the other planets?

4. Put the planets in alphabetical order. In alphabetical order, which planet comes in the exact middle?

The Planets

There are nine planets in our solar system.

MERCURY

Average distance from the Sun:
 36 million miles
Diameter: 3,032 miles
Temperature: 333 degrees F
Time to revolve around the Sun: 88 days
Time to rotate on its axis:
58 days, 15 hours, 30 minutes
Number of moons: 0

DID YOU KNOW? *Four billion years ago a gigantic asteroid hit Mercury, creating a 1,300-mile-wide crater on the surface.*

VENUS

Average distance from the Sun:
 67 million miles
Diameter: 7,521 miles
Temperature: 867 degrees F
Time to revolve around the Sun:
 224.7 days
Time to rotate on its axis: 243 days
Number of moons: 0

DID YOU KNOW? *Even though Venus is farther away from the Sun than Mercury, it is the hottest planet because the high level of carbon dioxide in the atmosphere creates an extreme greenhouse effect.*

EARTH

Average distance from the Sun:
 93 million miles
Diameter: 7,926 miles
Temperature: −59 degrees F
Time to revolve around the Sun:
 365 1/4 days
Time to rotate on its axis: 23 hours,
 56 minutes, 4.2 seconds
Number of moons: 1

DID YOU KNOW? *The Earth is moving around the Sun at approximately 67,000 miles an hour.*

MARS

Average distance from the Sun:
 142 million miles
Diameter: 4,213 miles
Temperature: −81 degrees F
Time to revolve around the Sun:
 687 days
Time to rotate on its axis:
 24 hours, 37 minutes, 22 seconds
Number of moons: 2

DID YOU KNOW? *Many features on Mars seem to have been shaped by water, although the only water left on Mars is frozen underneath layers of dust at the north and south poles.*

JUPITER

Average distance from the Sun:
 484 million miles
Diameter: 88,732 miles
Temperature: −162 degrees F
Time to revolve around the Sun:
 11.9 years
Time to rotate on its axis: 9 hours,
 55 minutes, 30 seconds
Number of moons: 39

DID YOU KNOW? *Jupiter is so big that all the other planets in the solar system could fit inside it at the same time.*

SATURN

Average distance from the Sun:
 888 million miles
Diameter: 74,975 miles
Temperature: −218 degrees F
Time to revolve around the Sun:
 29.5 years
Time to rotate on its axis: 10 hours,
 30 minutes
Number of moons: 30

DID YOU KNOW? *Using the world's first telescope, the astronomer Galileo discovered a huge ring system around Saturn in 1610.*

URANUS

Average distance from the Sun:
 1.8 billion miles
Diameter: 31,763 miles
Temperature: −323 degrees F
Time to revolve around the Sun:
 84 years
Time to rotate on its axis: 17 hours,
 14 minutes
Number of moons: 21

DID YOU KNOW? *Viewed from a telescope on Earth, Uranus appears to rotate on its side because its poles are tilted 98 degrees.*

NEPTUNE

Average distance from the Sun:
 2.8 billion miles
Diameter: 30,603 miles
Temperature: −330 degrees F
Time to revolve around the Sun:
 164.8 years
Time to rotate on its axis: 16 hours,
 6 minutes
Number of moons: 8

DID YOU KNOW? *Winter on Triton, Neptune's largest satellite, is thought to be the coldest place in the solar system.*

PLUTO

Average distance from the Sun:
 3.6 billion miles
Diameter: 1,413 miles
Temperature: −369 degrees F
Time to revolve around the Sun:
 247.7 years
Time to rotate on its axis: 6 days,
 9 hours, 18 minutes
Number of moons: 1

DID YOU KNOW? *Every 228 years, Pluto's elliptical orbit brings it closer to the Sun than Neptune, for 20 years.*

QUESTIONS TO PONDER

1. Who discovered Saturn's rings?

2. Which planet is the hottest?

3. Each planet rotates on its axis at a different rate. List the planets in order from the fastest rotating planet to the slowest.

4. If there were a possibility of living creatures existing on any of the other eight planets, which planet do you think it would be? Give reasons to support your choice.

Our Moon

A moon is a natural satellite that orbits around a planet. Jupiter has 39 moons—more than any other planet in our solar system. By comparison, Earth has just one moon.

Earth's moon is about 238,900 miles from Earth. It is 2,160 miles in diameter and has no atmosphere. The dusty surface is covered with deep craters.

It takes the same time for the moon to rotate on its axis as it does to orbit Earth (27 days, 7 hours, 43 minutes). This is why one side of the moon is always facing Earth. The moon has no light of its own, but reflects light from the sun. The fraction of the lighted part of the moon that we can see on Earth is called a **phase**. It takes the moon about 29 ½ days to go through all of its phases.

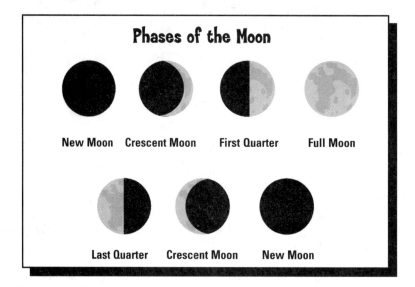

On July 20, 1969, Apollo 11's lunar module landed on the moon's surface in the area known as the Sea of Tranquility. American Neil Armstrong became the first person ever to walk on the moon. As he did so, he spoke the famous words: "That's one small step for man, one giant leap for mankind."

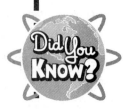

── QUESTIONS TO PONDER ──

1. How many more moons does Jupiter have than Earth?

2. Who was the first person to walk on the moon, and in what year did he accomplish this feat?

3. In the first paragraph, the moon is described as a "natural satellite." Can you think of any artificial satellites that orbit Earth? Name at least two and the functions each performs.

4. Pretend you are the first person to walk on the planet Mars. What words would you speak to describe the experience to the millions of people on Earth?

Space Words

There is a lot more to know about space and our solar system than just the planets. Here are a few words you might have heard before.

A **galaxy** is a group of billions of stars held together by gravity. Galaxies also contain interstellar gas and dust. The universe may have about 50 million galaxies. The one we live in is called the **Milky Way.** The sun and most stars we see are just a few of the 200 billion stars in the Milky Way.

A **light-year** is a measure of distance, not time. It is the distance light travels in a year going 186,000 miles per second—which is the fastest speed anything can travel. Alpha Centauri, the nearest star that we can see in the sky, is a little over four light-years away. When we see this star in the sky, the light we see is from four years ago!

Comets are fast-moving chunks of ice, dust, and rock that form huge gaseous heads as they move nearer to the sun. One of the most well-known is Halley's Comet. It can be seen about every 76 years and will appear in the sky again in the year 2061.

Asteroids (or minor planets) are solid chunks of rock or metal that range in size from small boulders to hundreds of miles across. Thousands of asteroids orbit the sun between Mars and Jupiter.

Satellites are objects that move in an orbit around a planet. Moons are natural satellites. Satellites made by humans are used as space stations and observatories. They are also used to take pictures of Earth's surface and to transmit communication signals.

Meteoroids are small pieces of stone or metal traveling in space. Most meteoroids are fragments from comets or asteroids that broke off from crashes in space with other objects.

WHAT IS AN ECLIPSE

During a **solar eclipse,** the moon casts a shadow on Earth. A total solar eclipse is when the sun is completely blocked out. When this happens, a halo of gas can be seen around the sun. This is called the **corona**.

Sometimes Earth casts a shadow on the moon. During a total **lunar eclipse,** the moon remains visible, but it looks dark, often with a reddish tinge (from sunlight bent through Earth's atmosphere).

QUESTIONS TO PONDER

1. What is the name of our galaxy?
2. *Complete this sentence*: During a _____ eclipse, the moon is between Earth and the sun.
3. A space station would be an example of a _____.
   a. asteroid   b. satellite   c. meteoroid
4. How old will you be when Halley's Comet next appears in the sky?

Batter Up!

How much do you know about the sport that has often been called "America's pastime"? Here are a few cool feats, facts, and firsts from the sport of baseball:

► With 64 homers in 2001, Sammy Sosa became the only player ever to hit more than 60 in a season three times.

► The youngest major leaguer in the modern era was Cincinnati Reds pitcher Joe Nuxhall, who made his debut in 1944 at the age of 15 years, 10 months, and 11 days.

► The youngest player in the modern era to hit a home run was Tommy Brown (17 years, 4 months, 14 days) of the Brooklyn Dodgers. He hit it against the Pirates in 1945.

► The most total runs ever scored in a game is 49. The Chicago Cubs beat the Philadelphia Phillies 26–23 in 1922.

► Joel Youngblood is the only major leaguer to get a hit for two different teams on the same day. In 1982, while playing for the Mets in an afternoon game in Chicago, he was told he'd been traded to the Expos. He left during the game and flew to Philadelphia, where he played that evening.

► Little League Baseball is the largest youth sports program in the world. It began in 1939 in Williamsport, Pennsylvania, with 45 boys playing on three teams. Now nearly three million boys and girls ages 5 to 18 play on 200,000 Little League teams in more than 80 countries.

► Pete Gray, a man with only one arm, played in 77 games for the St. Louis Browns in 1945.

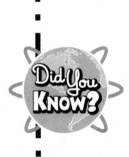

In the early 20th century Major League Baseball, like America, was segregated. Black and Latino players weren't allowed in the majors. They formed their own teams and traveled around, playing exhibition games against each other and any other teams they could find. This was called "barnstorming." Famous players included Josh Gibson, a powerful home run hitter called the "black Babe Ruth"; James "Cool Papa" Bell, a base-stealer said to be so fast he could "turn out the light and get in bed before the room got dark"; and the legendary Leroy "Satchel" Paige, who pitched into his 50s. Hall of Fame players like Hank Aaron, Roy Campanella, and Willie Mays got their start in the Negro Leagues.

——— QUESTIONS TO PONDER ———

1. Who is the only player to hit more than 60 home runs in a season three times?

2. What does the word *segregated* mean?

3. On average, how many boys played on each of the three 1939 Williamsport, Pennsylvania, Little League Baseball teams?

    a. 9   b. 15   c. 45

4. Did you notice that from 1944–1945, these unusual events occurred: the youngest player ever played in a game, a very young player hit a home run, and a man with one arm played major league baseball? During the mid 1940s, many men who might not have normally gotten a chance to play major league baseball were allowed to play. Why do you think that happened?

Football's Fantastic Finishes

American football began as a college sport in 1875. Almost 50 years later, the National Football League (NFL) was formed and has since become a very popular American pastime. In 1967, the NFL began calling its championship game the Super Bowl. Now, several Super Bowls have been among the most-watched events in television history. One reason football games are so popular are their knack for having exciting endings. Here are a few memorable games from NFL history.

"The Greatest Game Ever Played" December 28, 1958, NFL Championship, New York, New York (Yankee Stadium): Baltimore Colts 23, New York Giants 17. With a 14-3 lead in the 3rd quarter, the Colts had the ball on the Giants' 1-yard line and seemed to be on their way to an easy win. But the Giants made a goal-line stand, got the ball on their own 5-yard line, and drove downfield for a TD. In the 4th quarter, Frank Gifford caught a TD pass to give the Giants a 17-14 lead. But Colts star quarterback Johnny Unitas passed his team down the field. With seven seconds left, the Colts kicked a field goal to force the first post-season overtime. In the extra period, Unitas took the Colts 80 yards before fullback Alan Ameche bulled into the end zone from the 1-yard line to end what many still call "the greatest game ever played."

"The Immaculate Reception" December 23, 1972, AFC Divisional Playoffs, Pittsburgh, Pennsylvania: Pittsburgh Steelers 13, Oakland Raiders 7. Down 7-6, the Steelers' Terry Bradshaw fired a pass downfield to halfback John Fuqua, who was hit hard by Raiders defender Jack Tatum just as the ball arrived. It hit one of the players and bounced in the air and, luckily for the Steelers, into the hands of rookie running back Franco Harris. After his "immaculate reception," Harris ran 42 yards to score with five seconds left.

"The Catch" January 10, 1982, NFC Championship Game, San Francisco, California: San Francisco 49ers 28, Dallas Cowboys 27. The 49ers and Cowboys traded the lead six times. With less than five minutes to go and behind 27-21, the 49ers got the ball on their own 11-yard line. Led by quarterback Joe Montana, the Niners were able to move the ball to the Cowboys' six-yard line with 58 seconds left. Montana connected with receiver Dwight Clark, whose now-famous leaping catch for the winning TD sent the 49ers to their first Super Bowl.

"The Comeback" January 3, 1993, AFC Wild Card Game, Orchard Park, New York: Buffalo Bills 41, Houston Oilers 38 (OT). Down 35-3 early in the third quarter, Buffalo backup quarterback Frank Reich (starter Jim Kelly was injured) went to work. The Bills scored an amazing five straight TDs to go ahead 38-35. Houston's Al Del Greco tied the game with a field goal as the fourth quarter ended. In overtime, Buffalo's Nate Odomes picked off a Warren Moon pass. That set up Steve Christie's field goal to end one of the NFL's greatest comebacks.

Every time wide receiver Jerry Rice catches a pass or touchdown (TD), he sets a new record. At the end of the 2002 season, Rice had scored 202 TDs in his 18-year career, including a record 192 receiving TDs. He has caught over 350 more passes than any other NFL receiver.

━━ QUESTIONS TO PONDER ━━

1. What does NFL stand for?
2. Who threw "The Catch"?
3. How many total points were scored in the game nicknamed "The Comeback"? (Hint: a field goal is worth 3 points.)

   a. 38   b. 73   c. 79

4. Football is a fairly violent sport, and players often get injured. If you were Jerry Rice and you had already accomplished so much in your NFL career, would you choose to retire now or would you want to keep playing? Explain your answer.

The World's Sport

Soccer, also called football outside of the U.S., is the number-one sport worldwide. It is played by the most people, and it is played in almost every country. More than 240 million people play organized soccer, according to a 2000 survey done by FIFA (Federation Internationale de Football Association), the sport's international governing body. Look at that number one more time: 240 million—that's one out of every 25 persons on Earth! Here is a listing of a few of the countries that have the highest number of regular adult soccer (football) players.

Country	Number of Soccer Players
United States	18 million
Indonesia	10 million
Mexico	7.4 million
China	7.2 million
Brazil	7 million
Germany	6.3 million

Held every four years, the Men's World Cup is the biggest soccer tournament in the world. The first World Cup was held in Uruguay in 1930. In 1998 the World Cup competition was held in France. It was estimated that more than two billion people—one out of every three people on Earth—watched the final game that year between Brazil and France, which won 3-0.

QUESTIONS TO PONDER

1. What is FIFA?

2. When you write out 240 million in numeric form, how many zeroes do you have to write?

3. Using the information given on this page about the World Cup, about how many people are there on Earth?

     a. 6 billion   b. 2 billion   c. 240 million

4. Why do you think soccer is the most popular sport worldwide? Give at least two reasons.

Lord Stanley's Cup

Ice hockey began in Canada in the mid 1800s, and the National Hockey League (NHL) formed in 1916. Each year, the NHL's top two teams compete in a championship series. The winner gets to take home Lord Stanley's Cup—really! Each member of the winning team actually gets to take home the huge, famous trophy for a day. Here's the story of the Cup.

In 1892, Lord Stanley, the British governor general of Canada, bought a silver cup (actually a bowl) as an annual prize for the best amateur hockey team in Canada.

Today, NHL champions have their names engraved on one of the silver rings around the cup's base. When all the bands are filled, the oldest one is retired to the Hockey Hall of Fame and a new ring is added.

The Stanley Cup is the only professional sports trophy that each player on the winning team gets to take home. The Cup has had many interesting adventures:

► In 1997, Darren McCarty of the Red Wings took the cup to Bob's Big Boy for breakfast, then for a round of golf in the afternoon.

► In 2000, New Jersey's Scott Gomez rode with the cup to his hometown of Anchorage, Alaska, on a dogsled. Later that summer, one of Gomez's teammates, goalie Martin Brodeur, brought it to the movies and filled it with popcorn.

► In 2001, Mark Waggoner (Avalanche vice president of finance) took the trophy to new heights. With a special backpack, he carried the 35-pound cup up 14,433 feet to the top of Colorado's highest mountain (Mount Elbert).

The New York Rangers won the Stanley Cup in 1940—and then had to wait until 1994 before they were able to win it again!

━━ QUESTIONS TO PONDER ━━

1. What is most different about the Stanley Cup compared to other professional sports trophies?

2. How many years did the New York Rangers have to wait between winning the Stanley Cup?

3. How old was the bowl of the Stanley Cup when Martin Brodeur filled it with popcorn at the movies?

4. Where would you take the Stanley Cup if you could have it for one day?

Same Distance, Different Times

What would people from the 1600s, or the 1800s, think if they could come back and look at the world today? They would get lots of surprises. One surprise would be how fast people can travel to distant places.

The following timeline describes several famous trips and the times it took to complete them.

1620	*The Mayflower* took 66 days to sail across the Atlantic from Plymouth, England, to present-day Provincetown, Massachusetts.
1819	The first Atlantic Ocean crossing by a ship powered in part by steam (*Savannah*, from Savannah, Georgia, to Liverpool, England) took 27 days.
1845	A trip from Missouri to California by "wagon train" (covered wagons, usually pulled by oxen) took 4–5 months.
1854	The clipper ship *Flying Cloud* sailed from New York to San Francisco (going around the tip of South America) in a record 89 days, 8 hours.
1876	The *Transcontinental Express*, celebrating the U.S. centennial, crossed the country by rail from New York to San Francisco, in a record 83 hours, 39 minutes.
1927	Charles Lindbergh flew from New York to Paris in 33½ hours. It was the first nonstop flight made across the Atlantic by one person.
1952	The passenger ship *United States* set a record when it crossed the Atlantic in 3 days, 10 hours, and 40 minutes.
1969	Apollo 11, averaging 3,417 mph, took just under four days to reach the moon (about 70 times the distance from London to New York).
1981	At a speed of about 17,500 miles per hour, space shuttle *Columbia* circled the globe in 90 minutes.
1990	A U.S. Air Force SR-71 "Blackbird" flew coast-to-coast in 1 hour, 7 minutes, and 54 seconds (at an average speed of 2,124 miles per hour).
1995	Two Air Force B-1B bombers flew around the world nonstop (refueling in flight) in 36 hours and 13 minutes.
1996	A British Airways Concorde jet flew from New York to London in 2 hours, 53 minutes.
1999	Bertrand Piccard and Brian Jones completed the first around-the-world balloon flight in the *Breitling Orbiter 3*. It took 19 days, 21 hours, 55 minutes.
2002	Steve Fossett sailed across the Atlantic from New York to Cornwall, England. It took 4 days, 17 hours, 28 minutes.

——— QUESTIONS TO PONDER ———

1. About how many days did it take Apollo 11 to reach the moon?

2. What does the word transcontinental mean?

3. Look at the voyages from New York to San Francisco that took place in both 1854 and 1876. About how many more days did it take to sail in 1854 than it took to go by train in 1876?

   a. 6 days   b. 36 days   c. 86 days

4. What do you think a time traveler from the 1800s would find most surprising about our 21st-century world?

The Automobile

Probably no single type of vehicle affects your day-to-day life more than the automobile. Do you know the history behind the four-wheeled wonder that gets you to school and your parents to work each and every day?

In 1886 **Gottlieb Daimler** patented a three-wheeled motor carriage in Germany. That same year, **Karl Benz** produced his first successful gasoline-powered vehicle. **John W. Lambert** of Ohio made the first gas-powered automobile in the U.S. in 1891.

Five years later, the **Duryea Brothers** of Springfield, Massachusetts, started the first car manufacturing company in the U.S. **Henry Ford** came soon after. His production of the Model T using an assembly line in 1913 revolutionized the automobile industry, making cars affordable for large numbers of people. Many improvements were made over the years, such as the first aerodynamically designed car, the **Chrysler Airflow** (1934); and air-conditioning, introduced by the Packard company in 1940. Ferdinand Porsche's **Volkswagen** "beetle," mass-produced after World War II, was one of the most popular cars in history.

Today's cars have computer-run features that make them safer and more efficient. Some even have the Global Positioning System to help you get where you want to go. But the main focus for developing the car of the future is fuel efficiency. Scientists all over the world are working on designing alternative-fuel cars. **Zero Emission Vehicles** (ZEVs) that use hydrogen cells to make electricity are one promising possibility.

———— QUESTIONS TO PONDER ————

1. Which American automobile manufacturer introduced the Model T in 1913?

2. What are ZEVs? According to the article above, what is the main focus for developing this car of the future?

3. How did Henry Ford's development of the assembly line in 1913 allow him to build more cars at a more affordable price?

4. Have you thought about what type of car you would like to own when you are old enough to drive? Do you think it will be important to you to have an expensive car, or would you just want a car that is dependable and affordable?

A Short History of Transportation

5000 B.C.
People harness animal-muscle power. Oxen and donkeys carry heavy loads.

3500 B.C.
Egyptians create the first sailboat. Before this, people made rafts or canoes and paddled them with poles or their hands.

1450s
Portuguese build fast ships with three masts. These plus the compass usher in an age of exploration.

1730s
Stagecoach service begins in the U.S.

5000 B.C.

3500 B.C.
In Mesopotamia (modern-day Iraq), people invent vehicles with wheels. But the first wheels are made of heavy wood, and the roads are terrible.

1100 B.C.
Chinese invent the magnetic compass. It allows them to sail long distances.

1660s
Horse-drawn stagecoaches begin running in France. They stop at stages to switch horses and passengers—the first mass transit system.

1769
James Watt patents the first successful steam engine.

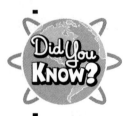

Did You Know?

The California Gold Rush of 1849 made people realize the need to build a railroad to speed the trip from California to the east. In 1862 Congress authorized funds to build the railroad. The Union Pacific was to build west from Omaha, Nebraska, and the Central Pacific was to build east from Sacramento, California. From 1866–1869, the two companies struggled to overcome rugged terrain, desert heat, freezing winters, and hostile attacks. Finally, in 1869, the two roads were joined at Promontory Point in Utah. A golden spike was driven into the last tie to commemorate this milestone.

A Short History of Transportation *(cont.)*

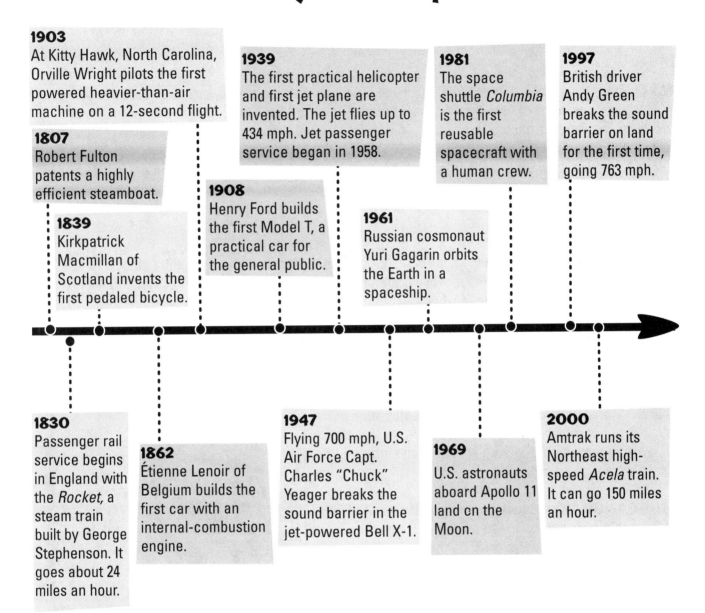

1903
At Kitty Hawk, North Carolina, Orville Wright pilots the first powered heavier-than-air machine on a 12-second flight.

1807
Robert Fulton patents a highly efficient steamboat.

1839
Kirkpatrick Macmillan of Scotland invents the first pedaled bicycle.

1939
The first practical helicopter and first jet plane are invented. The jet flies up to 434 mph. Jet passenger service began in 1958.

1908
Henry Ford builds the first Model T, a practical car for the general public.

1981
The space shuttle *Columbia* is the first reusable spacecraft with a human crew.

1961
Russian cosmonaut Yuri Gagarin orbits the Earth in a spaceship.

1997
British driver Andy Green breaks the sound barrier on land for the first time, going 763 mph.

1830
Passenger rail service begins in England with the *Rocket,* a steam train built by George Stephenson. It goes about 24 miles an hour.

1862
Étienne Lenoir of Belgium builds the first car with an internal-combustion engine.

1947
Flying 700 mph, U.S. Air Force Capt. Charles "Chuck" Yeager breaks the sound barrier in the jet-powered Bell X-1.

1969
U.S. astronauts aboard Apollo 11 land on the Moon.

2000
Amtrak runs its Northeast high-speed *Acela* train. It can go 150 miles an hour.

QUESTIONS TO PONDER

1. People from which country invented the compass?

   a. U.S.   b. Japan   c. China

2. The two end points of the railroad constructed in the western U.S. in the 1860s were Sacramento, California, and Omaha, Nebraska. Which city, Sacramento or Omaha, is now the capital of its state?

3. A person who lived on the continent of _____ invented the first pedaled bicycle.

   a. Europe   b. Asia   c. North America

4. Which of the inventions and advancements on the time line above do you feel is the most important? Explain your answer.

World Cities

The world is a diverse place, with all kinds of places to see and cities to visit. Here are a few of the great cities the world has to offer.

AMSTERDAM—Ride your way through a maze of **canals** on a pedal boat called a "canal bike," or rent a regular bicycle on streets that are great for cycling. The **Anne Frank House**, where the Frank family went into hiding from the Nazis in World War II, is now a world-renowned museum.

LONDON—Ride the **double-decker buses**—on the left side of the street!—from the ancient **Tower of London** to the sleek new Ferris wheel called the **London Eye**. And don't forget to visit some of the city's beautiful green spaces, such as **St. James's Park**.

NEW YORK—Take the elevator to the top of the **Empire State Building** for a bird's-eye view of this huge city. Get a look at the past when you walk through **South Street Seaport**. See the dinosaurs at the **Museum of Natural History**. Pet the real live zoo animals in **Central Park** and ride on the carousel. And don't forget the ferry to the **Statue of Liberty**.

PARIS—A short walk from the medieval cathedral of **Notre Dame** are the lively cafés of the **Left Bank**. After climbing the steps of Sacre Coeur in hilly **Montmartre**, enjoy a boat ride along the **Seine** or visit the **Eiffel Tower** and get a bird's-eye view of where you've been.

ROME—Pretend you're a gladiator at the **Colosseum** or explore the underground **Catacombs**. Back on the street, local artists are waiting to sketch your portrait at the **Piazza Navona**.

Colosseum in Rome, Italy

SAN FRANCISCO—Check out the **sea lions** at Pier 39, ride the **cable car** up through **Chinatown** and past the needle-like **Transamerica Pyramid**. Try the interactive exhibits at **Exploratorium**, a great museum of science, art, and technology. Finally, cross the bay on the **Golden Gate Bridge** and look back at the dramatic skyline.

TOKYO—If you're ready for an early-morning adventure, go for a dawn visit to the **Tsukiji Fish Market**. There are hundreds of fish types to see, and a bowl of steaming noodles will make a fun breakfast. Later in the day, see singing, dancing, and beautiful costumes at a **Kabuki theater**. There are also many beautiful **Buddhist temples** and **Shinto shrines** to visit.

━━━━━ QUESTIONS TO PONDER ━━━━━

1. In which city did Anne Frank and her family hide from the Nazis during World War II?

2. Through which of the cities listed on this page does the Seine river flow?

3. What are catacombs?

4. Which of the sites listed on this page would you most like to visit? Explain why.

Time Zones

Has this ever happened to you while you were traveling: it took you two hours to get somewhere, but when you got there the clocks all told you that it was three hours later? What happened? You just crossed a time zone.

What Are Time Zones?

A day is 24 hours long—the time it takes Earth to complete one rotation on its axis. Earth is divided into 24 time zones. Each zone is roughly 15 degrees of longitude wide.

The line of longitude passing through Greenwich, England, is the starting point. It is called the prime meridian. In the 12th time zone (and 180th meridian) the International Date Line appears. When you cross the line going west, it's tomorrow. Going east, you travel backward in time and the date is one day earlier.

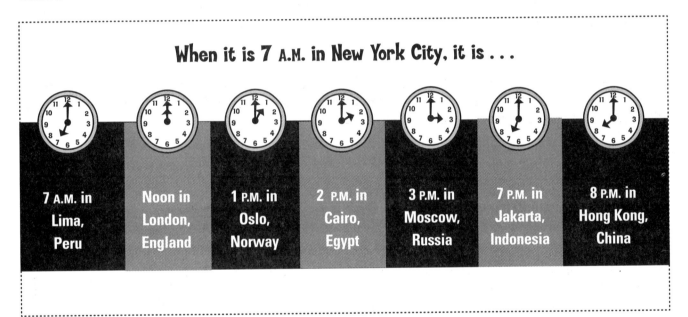

When it is 7 A.M. in New York City, it is . . .

| 7 A.M. in Lima, Peru | Noon in London, England | 1 P.M. in Oslo, Norway | 2 P.M. in Cairo, Egypt | 3 P.M. in Moscow, Russia | 7 P.M. in Jakarta, Indonesia | 8 P.M. in Hong Kong, China |

QUESTIONS TO PONDER

1. The prime meridian passes through which European city?

2. When it is noon in New York City, what time is it in Hong Kong, China?

3. Pretend you are in Moscow, Russia, celebrating New Year's Eve. The clock has just struck midnight. How many hours will it be before the people in New York City get to yell "Happy New Year!" to each other?

4. Is it possible to experience your birth date twice in one year? Explain how.

Amusement Parks

Amusement parks today are filled with bright lights, food, fun, and thrilling rides. But the earliest amusement parks, which appeared in Europe more than 400 years ago, were very different. Some of the attractions were flower gardens, bowling, music, and a few simple rides.

By 1884, amusement parks began to get more exciting. That's when the Switchback Gravity Pleasure Railway came to Coney Island in Brooklyn, New York. In 1893, the George Ferris Great Wheel was introduced in Chicago. The "Ferris" Wheel weighed more than four million pounds and stood 264 feet high. A year later, Chutes Park opened in Chicago. It was the first park to charge admission.

In the 1920s, some of the best roller coasters of all time were built. Many large cities had as many as six amusement parks. But the stock market crash and the Great Depression in the 1930s caused many parks to close.

In 1955, Disneyland opened in Anaheim, California. Different sections of the park, such as Tomorrowland and Frontierland, had their own themes. Disneyland became known as the country's first theme park.

These days amusement parks are more popular than ever, with thrill-seekers flocking to places like Six-Flags Great Adventure in New Jersey. Those with strong stomachs can brave the sleek, ultramodern, gravity-defying rides like Medusa, while others can stick to less scary kinds of fun.

- ▶ **The Africa Safari Park** near Baton Rouge, LA, lets you get a look at exotic species from all over the world. While riding in your car along the gravel road, you can stop to meet and even feed the animals.
- ▶ **Bonfante Gardens Theme Park** in Gilroy, CA, has a collection of weird "circus trees." Their trunks might form the shape of a basket, or a lightning bolt, or a huge piece of jewelry. This is done by pruning, grafting, and bending the trees as they grow. Each tree is really several trees that have grown together to look like one.
- ▶ At **Legoland** in Carlsbad, CA (and in Europe), Lego blocks are used to make everything from cities to cars to driver's licenses. It's a whole new world made out of blocks just like the ones you might have at home.
- ▶ **SeaWorld** (with locations in San Antonio, TX, San Diego, CA, and Orlando, FL) is the home of all kinds of exciting marine life, from friendly porpoises to killer whales!

━━━━━ QUESTIONS TO PONDER ━━━━━

1. In what year did Disneyland open?

2. What event in U.S. history led to the closing of several amusement parks in the 1930s?

3. At which amusement park listed above could you visit an aquarium?

4. As you have read, amusement parks can be based on all kinds of themes—from Disney characters to marine life to strange trees. If you could design an amusement park, what theme would you base it on?

Roller Coasters

Did you know that America's first roller coaster wasn't supposed to be fun at all?

It was built in 1827 to carry coal from a Pennsylvania mountaintop mine to boats on the canal below. But the speeding coal carts of "Gravity Road" soon attracted crowds. The owners agreed to let people (including commuters) ride in the afternoons, with mornings still reserved for coal. Gravity Road's rails are gone now, but they ran for 18 miles and dropped a total of more than 1,200 feet—more than any roller coaster built just for fun.

Now take a look at some of the world's fastest, longest, and tallest roller coasters. How would you like to ride all of these in one day?

WORLD'S FASTEST ROLLER COASTERS

1. *Top Thrill Dragster:* 120 mph, Sandusky, Ohio
2. *Dodonpa:* 107 mph, Gotemba City, Japan
3. *Superman: The Escape:* 100 mph, Valencia, California
4. *Steel Dragon 2000:* 95 mph, Mie, Japan
5. *Millennium Force:* 92 mph, Sandusky, Ohio

WORLD'S LONGEST ROLLER COASTERS

1. *Steel Dragon 2000:* 8,133 ft, Mie, Japan
2. *The Ultimate:* 7,498 ft, North Yorkshire, England
3. *The Beast:* 7,400 ft, Cincinnati, Ohio
4. *Son of Beast:* 7,032 ft, Cincinnati, Ohio
5. *Millennium Force:* 6,595 ft, Sandusky, Ohio

WORLD'S TALLEST ROLLER COASTERS

1. *Top Thrill Dragster:* 420 ft, Sandusky, Ohio
2. *Superman: The Escape:* 415 ft, Valencia, California
3. *Tower of Terror:* 380 ft, Gold Coast, Australia
4. *Steel Dragon 2000:* 318 ft, Mie, Japan
5. *Fujiyama:* 259 ft, Yamanashi, Japan

━ QUESTIONS TO PONDER ━

1. In what state was America's first roller coaster?

2. What percentage of the world's five longest roller coasters are in Ohio?

3. If you wanted to ride a roller coaster that was the best combination of the fastest, longest, and tallest roller coaster in the world, which one roller coaster from the lists above would you ride?

4. If you love riding roller coasters, explain what it is about them that you enjoy. If you hate roller coasters, explain why.

The U.S. Constitution

The Constitution is a document that created the present government of the United States. It was written in 1787 and went into effect in 1789. It establishes the three branches of the U.S. government, which are the executive (headed by the president), the legislative (the Congress), and the judicial (the Supreme Court and other federal courts).

The Constitution begins with a short statement called the Preamble. The Preamble states that the government of the United States was established by the people.

> **"We, the people of the United States, in order to form a more perfect Union, establish justice, insure domestic tranquility, provide for the common defense, promote the general welfare, and secure the blessings of liberty to ourselves and our posterity do ordain and establish this Constitution for the United States of America."**

Amendments to the Constitution

The writers of the Constitution understood that it might need to be amended, or changed, in the future. In order for an amendment to be passed, it must be approved by two-thirds of the legislative branch (the House and Senate) and three-fourths of the states. Thus far, the Constitution has been amended 27 times. The first 10 amendments are known as the Bill of Rights. Here is a summary of them:

1	Guarantees freedom of religion, speech, and the press	**6**	Guarantees people accused of crimes the right to a speedy public trial by jury
2	Guarantees the right of the people to have firearms	**7**	Guarantees people the right to a trial by jury for other kinds of cases
3	Guarantees that soldiers cannot be lodged in private homes unless the owner agrees	**8**	Prohibits "cruel and unusual punishments"
4	Protects citizens against being searched or having their property searched or taken away by the government without a good reason	**9**	Says that specific rights listed in the Constitution do not take away rights that may not be listed
5	Protects rights of people on trial for crimes	**10**	Establishes that any powers not given specifically to the federal government belong to states or the people

QUESTIONS TO PONDER

1. The short statement that begins the U.S. Constitution is called the _____.
   - a. Bill of Rights
   - b. 1st Amendment
   - c. Preamble

2. The Preamble mentions that part of the purpose of the Constitution is to "insure domestic tranquility." Which of the following is a synonym for the word tranquility?
   - a. peace
   - b. war
   - c. justice

3. How many states must approve an amendment in order for it to pass?

4. Which of the first 10 amendments to the Constitution do you think is the most important? Explain your answer.

U.S. Supreme Court

The highest court in the United States is the Supreme Court. It has nine justices who are appointed for life by the president with the approval of the Senate. Eight of the nine members are called associate justices. The ninth is the chief justice, who presides over the Court's meetings.

What Does the Supreme Court Do?

The Supreme Court's major responsibilities are to judge cases that involve reviewing federal laws, actions of the president, treaties of the United States, and laws passed by state governments to be sure they do not conflict with the U.S. Constitution. If the Supreme Court finds that a law or action violates the Constitution, the law is struck down.

The Supreme Court's Decision Is Final.

Most cases must go through other state courts or federal courts before they reach the Supreme Court. The Supreme Court is the final court for a case, and the justices decide which cases they will review. After the Supreme Court hears a case, it may agree or disagree with the decision by a lower court. When the Supreme Court makes a ruling, its decision is final. In December 2000, the Supreme Court made a decision that meant George W. Bush was the winner of the November election for president.

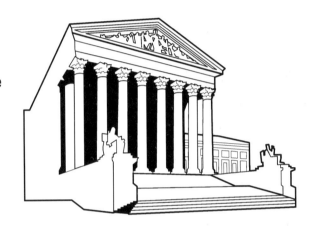

SUPREME COURT HANDSHAKE *Every day before they go into court and at the start of their private conferences where they discuss cases together, each justice shakes hands with the other eight. Justice Melville W. Fuller started this practice in the late 1800s. He wanted the justices to remember that, despite differences of opinion, they all share the same purpose.*

━ QUESTIONS TO PONDER ━

1. How many justices are there on the U.S. Supreme Court?

2. If the Supreme Court disagrees with a law of a state government, what happens?

3. What does the Supreme Court handshake symbolize?

4. Do you think that a court that is the final say in all legal and Constitutional matters and whose members are appointed for life is a good or bad idea? Explain your answer.

Famous African Americans

The people below fought racial barriers in order to achieve their goals.

ARTHUR ASHE (1943–1993) won the U.S. Open in tennis (1968), and became the first black member of the U.S. Davis Cup team. In 1975 he won Wimbledon and was ranked #1 in the world. Off the court, he was a critic of racial injustice and helped promote awareness of AIDS, a disease he got from a blood transfusion following heart surgery.

CONDOLEEZZA RICE (born 1954) is the first African American, and the first woman, to be National Security Advisor, who gives the U.S. president advice on foreign and defense policy. She is an expert on Eastern Europe and was a professor and top official at Stanford University in California.

THURGOOD MARSHALL (1908–1993) became the first African-American justice on the U.S. Supreme Court in 1967. In 1954, he won a historic case, *Brown v. Board of Education of Topeka*, before the Supreme Court. The Court ruled that separate schools for black and white students were not equal or legal.

COLIN POWELL (born 1937) became the first African-American U.S. secretary of state in 2001. In 1991, while serving as the first black chairman of the Joint Chiefs of Staff, he oversaw Operation Desert Storm in the Persian Gulf War.

A. PHILIP RANDOLPH (1889–1979) was a labor leader and civil rights activist. In 1925 he organized the Brotherhood of Sleeping Car Porters, the first union of mainly black workers to be recognized by the American Federation of Labor. He helped persuade President Franklin D. Roosevelt to create the Fair Employment Practices Committee in 1941. He was elected vice-president of the AFL-CIO in 1957.

REVEREND MARTIN LUTHER KING JR. (1929–1968) used his forceful speaking style, forceful personality, and belief in nonviolence to help change U.S. history. From the mid 1950s to his assassination in 1968, he was the most influential leader of the U.S. civil rights movement.

JACKIE ROBINSON (1919–1972) was the first black player in the history of Major League Baseball. He joined the Dodgers (then in Brooklyn) in 1947. In 1949 he won the National Leagues MVP award; and in 1962 he was elected to the Baseball Hall of Fame.

HARRIET TUBMAN (1821–1913) escaped slavery when she was in her twenties. Before the Civil War, she repeatedly risked her life to lead hundreds of slaves to freedom by way of a network of homes and churches called the "Underground Railroad."

QUESTIONS TO PONDER

1. Who was the first woman to serve as U.S. National Security Advisor?
2. In what year was Jackie Robinson elected to the Baseball Hall of Fame?
   a. 1947   b. 1949   c. 1962
3. What was the Underground Railroad?
4. Reverend Martin Luther King Jr.'s birthday was first officially observed as a national holiday in the U.S. in 1986. Do you think there are any famous Americans whose birthdays aren't observed as national holidays but should be? Name one, and make a case for why his or her birthday should be a national holiday.

National Parks

The world's first national park was Yellowstone, established in 1872 in Wyoming. Since then, the U.S. government has set aside 54 other national parks. Here's your chance to get to know more about three of America's treasured national parks.

EVERGLADES NATIONAL PARK is a swampy, subtropical wilderness at the southwestern tip of Florida. It was created in 1934 especially to preserve the varied plant and animal life there. Most of the 1,399,078 acres are covered by shallow water during the wet season—one reason why the Everglades are called the "river of grass." There are 300 species of birds, 120 kinds of trees, 25 varieties of orchids, and 1,000 kinds of other plants. Thirty-six endangered animal species live there, including alligators, crocodiles, Florida panthers, and manatees, also known as sea cows. The manatees are sea creatures with thick gray skin. They are big (they can be 15 feet long and can weigh up to 1,200 pounds), but they are very gentle.

SEQUOIA AND KINGS CANYON NATIONAL PARK, founded in 1890, is the second oldest national park (after Yellowstone). Located in central California, it is home to the world's largest living thing, the General Sherman Tree. At 275 feet tall, this giant sequoia is not the tallest of all trees, but it is the most massive. It measures 102 feet round at the base of the trunk and weighs some 1,385 tons! The park is also the location of Mount Whitney, the highest peak in the United States outside Alaska, at 14,494 feet. Visitors to the park can take a guided tour of the Crystal Cave, a marble cavern with many rock formations.

YOSEMITE NATIONAL PARK, established in 1890, covers 761,266 acres in east-central California. It has the world's largest concentration of granite domes—mountain-like rocks that were created by glaciers millions of years ago. You can see many of them rising thousands of feet above the valley floor. Two of the most famous are Half-Dome, which looks smooth and rounded, and El Capitan, which is the biggest single granite rock on earth. Skilled climbers come from all over the world to scale this 4,000-foot-high wall of rock. Yosemite Falls, which drops 2,425 feet, is the highest waterfall in North America, and the fifth highest in the world. It is actually two waterfalls, called the upper and lower falls, connected by a series of smaller waterfalls. Yosemite also features lakes, meadows, and giant sequoia trees, and is home to bighorn sheep and bears.

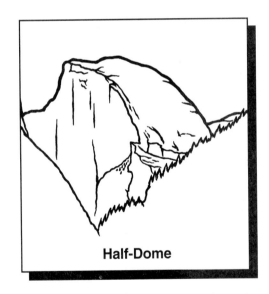

Half-Dome

QUESTIONS TO PONDER

1. What is the name of the biggest single granite rock on Earth?

2. If you wanted to see a sea cow, which of the national parks on this page would you visit?

3. Put the three national parks listed on this page in order of when they were established, from first to last.

4. The population in the United States is constantly growing, which forces many areas to become more and more crowded. Even so, do you feel that preserving some land from civilization is important to our nation? Why or why not?

Measuring Temperature

When the weather is really hot or really cold, people usually ask one question: "How hot [or cold] is it today?" What they want to hear is a number. It's the way we express the heat or the cold.

Two systems for measuring temperature are used in weather forecasting. One is Fahrenheit (abbreviated F). The other is Celsius (abbreviated C). Zero degrees (0°) Celsius is equal to 32° Fahrenheit.

TO CONVERT FAHRENHEIT TEMPERATURES TO CELSIUS:

(1) Subtract 32 from the Fahrenheit temperature value.

(2) Then multiply by 5.

(3) Then divide the result by 9.

Example: To convert 68 degrees Fahrenheit to Celsius, 68 − 32 = 36; 36 x 5 = 180; 180 ÷ 9 = 20

TO CONVERT CELSIUS TEMPERATURES TO FAHRENHEIT:

(1) Multiply the Celsius temperature by 9.

(2) Then divide by 5.

(3) Then add 32 to the result.

Example: To convert 20 degrees Celsius to Fahrenheit,

20 x 9 = 180; 180 ÷ 5 = 36; 36 + 32 = 68

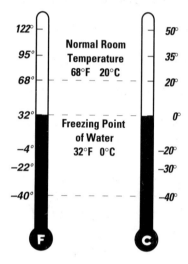

Here is a list of the hottest and coldest temperatures ever recorded on each of the continents.

CONTINENT	HIGHEST TEMPERATURE	LOWEST TEMPERATURE
Africa	El Azizia, Libya, 136°F (58°C)	Ifrane, Morocco, −11°F (−24°C)
Antarctica	Vanda Station, 59°F (15°C)	Vostok, −129°F (−89°C)
Asia	Tirat Tsvi, Israel, 129°F (54°C)	Verkhoyansk, Russia, and Oimekon, Russia, −90°F (−68°C)
Australia	Cloncurry, Queensland, 128°F (53°C)	Charlotte Pass, New South Wales, −9°F (−23°C)
Europe	Seville, Spain, 122°F (50°C)	Ust'Shchugor, Russia, −67°F (−55°C)
North America	Death Valley, California, 134°F (57°C)	Snag, Yukon Territory, −81°F (−63°C)
South America	Rivadavia, Argentina, 120°F (49°C)	Sarmiento, Argentina, −27°F (−33°C)

QUESTIONS TO PONDER

1. What was the hottest temperature ever recorded in the United States?

2. What is the only temperature at which the two temperature systems meet?

3. How many degrees Fahrenheit is 10°C?

4. Which system do you think is easier to use: Fahrenheit or Celsius? Explain your answer.

Wet and Windy Weather

Depending on where you live, the weather is not always nice and sunny. There are many different ways in which the weather can get you wet or mess up your hair. Here are a few:

BLIZZARD—A heavy snowstorm with strong winds.

FREEZING RAIN—Water that freezes as it hits the ground.

HAIL—Water droplets that get coated with ice as they are blown upward into colder temperatures, often again and again. As they get heavy they fall to the ground as hailstones.

PRECIPITATION—Water that falls from clouds as rain, snow, hail, or sleet.

RAIN—Water falling in drops.

SLEET—Water that reaches the ground as ice pellets or a mixture of snow and rain.

SNOW—Small white ice crystals that form in clouds and fall.

TORNADO—A violently rotating column of air (wind) that forms a funnel. A tornado can suck up and destroy what is in its path, and also cause severe damage from flying debris.

HURRICANES—are the largest storms. They form over warm, usually tropical, oceans. As the warm seawater evaporates into the air, the pressure drops and winds begin to circulate, creating a huge wall of clouds and rain, wrapped around a calm center. As warm, moist air continues to feed the storm, it gets stronger and can spread out to an area 300 miles wide. Winds up to 250 miles an hour can rip trees out by their roots and tear roofs off buildings. Torrential rains and giant waves caused by the fierce wind can cause flooding and massive damage before the storm finally moves out over land and dies down.

Hurricanes are named, and their names can be retired. Hurricane names come from a set of six lists that are used in turn, one list per year. But if a hurricane is particularly destructive, its name will be retired and never used again.

QUESTIONS TO PONDER

1. How fast can hurricane winds get?
   a. up to 25 mph   b. up to 250 mph   c. up to 2,500 mph

2. What is the general term given to water that falls from clouds?

3. Have you ever been caught in a blizzard or hurricane? Have you ever seen a tornado? Explain your experience.

4. Create a list of hurricane names. You need one name for each letter of the alphabet. Make sure half of the names are male names and the other half are female names.

Clouds

Clouds come from moisture in the atmosphere that cools and forms into tiny water droplets or ice crystals. The science of clouds is called nephology. The names we still use for clouds come from a lecture given in December 1802 by the English meteorologist Luke Howard. Here are some of the cloud types that he named:

ALTOSTRATUS CLOUDS form a smooth gray or bluish sheet high over the sky. The sun or moon can usually be seen faintly.

CIRROCUMULUS CLOUDS are high ice clouds with a wave-like or patchy appearance. The sunlight can make them look like fish scales, which makes for a "mackerel sky."

CIRRUS CLOUDS are thin, wispy, high-altitude clouds made of ice crystals. They often appear in nice weather.

CUMULONIMBUS CLOUDS, also known as storm clouds, are darkish and ominous-looking. They can bring heavy storms, often with thunder and lightning.

CUMULUS CLOUDS are puffy, white, vertical clouds that get biggest during mid afternoon. They form many different shapes.

NIMBOSTRATUS CLOUDS form a shapeless, dark layer across the sky, blocking out the sun and moon. They often bring a long period of rain or snow.

A barometer is an instrument that measures atmospheric pressure. Falling pressure means stormy weather, while rising pressure means calm weather.

QUESTIONS TO PONDER

1. Which clouds are thin, wispy, high-altitude clouds made of ice crystals?

2. If neph- is a prefix meaning "clouds," what do you think the suffix *–ology* means?

3. The article above says that cumulonimbus clouds are "darkish and ominous-looking." What does *ominous* mean?

4. What is your favorite type of weather? Do you know someone who likes a completely opposite type of weather? If so, why do you think that is?

Lightning

Have you ever wondered how lightning is created? Here's a quick explanation:

Cumulonimbus (thunder) clouds may stretch upward for miles, to where freezing temperatures turn the moisture in the cloud into **ice particles**. Those particles sink by gravity, then they rise with the cloud's air movement, and along the way they bump into each other and separate each other's electrical charges. The negatively charged ice particles drop lower down in the cloud and attract positive particles from the ground below: in lightning rods, trees, and anything else nearby. When the negative charges connect with the positive ones—zap!—there is a huge transfer of electricity, which we see as lightning. Lightning generates between 100 million and 1 billion volts of electricity and can heat the air around it to over 50,000°F. The rapid movement of air as it heats and cools makes the shockwaves you hear as thunder. Because light travels faster than sound, the thunder takes longer to reach your ears than the lightning does to reach your eyes. The sooner you hear thunder after lightning the closer the lightning is.

Being struck by lightning is unusual—but it happens! In the United States, lightning hits the earth an estimated 25 million times a year. On average, about 70 people in the U.S. are killed by lightning each year, and hundreds suffer injury. For safety, follow the "30-30 Rule": go indoors if you hear thunder 30 seconds or less after you see lightning, and don't go back out until 30 minutes after the last thunderclap.

By attaching a key to a kite string, Benjamin Franklin proved to the world that lightning is electricity and not some supernatural force. From there, Franklin went on to invent the lightning rod, a device that prevents lightning from striking and burning down buildings.

QUESTIONS TO PONDER

1. What sound does lightning cause?

2. How hot can the air around lightning get?

   a. 500°F   b. 5,000°F   c. 50,000°F

3. In addition to the lightning rod, Benjamin Franklin also invented bifocals. Bifocals are eyeglasses that are divided into more than one section so that the wearer can see different distances. Knowing what you know about number prefixes, how many sections are bifocals divided into?

4. Before Benjamin Franklin proved that lightning was electricity, people thought lightning was caused by supernatural force. Can you think of other things that people used to think were caused by supernatural force but that we now can prove scientifically?

The U.S. Customary System

The system of measurement used in the United States is called the U.S. customary system. Most other countries use the metric system. A few metric measurements are also used in the United States, such as for soda, which comes in one-liter and two-liter bottles. In the tables below, abbreviations are given in parentheses the first time they are used.

LENGTH, HEIGHT, and DISTANCE

The basic unit of length in the U.S. system is the inch. Length, width, depth, thickness, and the distance between two points all use the inch or larger related units.

1 foot (ft.) = 12 inches (in.)

1 yard (yd.) = 3 feet or 36 inches

1 rod (rd.) = 5½ yards

1 furlong (fur.) = 40 rods or 220 yards or 660 feet

1 mile (mi.) (also called statute mile) = 8 furlongs or 1,760 yards or 5,280 feet

1 league = 3 miles

AREA

Area is used to measure a section of a flat surface like the floor or the ground. Most area measurements are given in square units. Land is measured in acres.

1 square foot (sq. ft.) = 144 square inches (sq. in.)

1 square yard (sq. yd.) = 9 square feet or 1,296 square inches

1 square rod (sq. rd.) = 30 ¼ square yards

1 acre = 160 square rods or 4,840 square yards or 43,560 square feet

1 square mile (sq. mi.) = 640 acres

WEIGHT

Although 1 cubic foot of popcorn and 1 cubic foot of rock take up the same amount of space, they wouldn't feel the same if you tried to lift them. We measure heaviness as **weight**. Most objects are measured in **avoirdupois weight** (*pronounced* a-ver-de-POIZ), although precious metals and medicines use different systems.

1 dram (dr.) = 27.344 grains (gr.)

1 ounce (oz.) = 16 drams or 437.5 grains

1 pound (lb.) = 16 ounces

1 hundredweight (cwt.) = 100 pounds

1 ton = 2,000 pounds (also called short ton)

The U.S. Customary System *(cont.)*

CAPACITY

Units of **capacity** are used to measure how much of something will fit into a container. **Liquid measure** is used to measure liquids, such as water or gasoline. **Dry measure** is used with large amounts of solid materials, like grain or fruit.

Dry Measure Although both liquid and dry measures use the terms "pint" and "quart," they mean different amounts and should not be confused. Look at the lists below for examples.

1 quart (qt.) = 2 pints (pt.)   1 peck (pk.) = 8 quarts

1 bushel (bu.) = 4 pecks

Cooking Measurements Cooking measure is used to measure amounts of solid and liquid foods used in cooking. The measurements used in cooking are based on the **fluid ounce**.

1 teaspoon (tsp.) = ⅙ fluid ounce (fl. oz.)

1 tablespoon (tbsp.) = 3 teaspoons or ½ fluid ounce

1 cup = 16 tablespoons or 8 fluid ounces

1 pint = 2 cups

1 quart = 2 pints

1 gallon = 4 quarts

Liquid Measure Although the basic unit in liquid measure is the **gill** (4 fluid ounces), you are more likely to find liquids measured in pints or larger units.

1 gill = 4 fluid ounces

1 pint (pt.) = 4 gills or 16 ounces

1 quart (qt.) = 2 pints or 32 ounces

1 gallon (gal.) = 4 quarts = 128 ounces

For measuring most U.S. liquids,
    1 barrel (bbl.)   = 31½ gallons

For measuring oil, 1 barrel (bbl.) = 42 gallon

DEPTH

Some measurements of length are used to measure ocean depth and distance.

1 fathom = 6 feet

1 cable = 120 fathoms or 720 feet

1 nautical mile = 6,076.1 feet or
                    1.15 statute miles

VOLUME

The amount of space taken up by an object (or the amount of space available within an object) is measured in **volume**. Volume is usually expressed in **cubic units**. If you wanted to buy a room air conditioner and needed to know how much space there was to be cooled, you could measure the room in cubic feet.

1 cubic foot (cu. ft.) = 1,728 cubic inches (cu. in.)

1 cubic yard (cu. yd.) = 27 cubic feet

QUESTIONS TO PONDER

1. How many square inches are there in 2 square feet?

2. A pie recipe calls for 4 tablespoons of cinnamon, but you only have a teaspoon with which to measure. How many teaspoons of cinnamon do you put in your pie mixture?

3. Denver, Colorado, is known as the Mile High City. How high would you guess the elevation is in Denver?

    a. 640 acres   b. 1,280 square feet   c. 5,280 feet

4. Measure your height in inches. Then measure from fingertip to fingertip with your arms outstretched. Which measurement is greater? How does this compare with your classmates? Make a graph to show your findings.

The Metric System

Do you ever wonder how much soda you are getting when you buy a bottle that holds one liter? or do you wonder how long a 50-meter swimming pool is? or how far away from Montreal, Canada, you would be when a map says "8 kilometers"?

Every system of measurement uses a basic unit for measuring. In the U.S. customary system, the basic unit for length is the inch. In the metric system, the basic unit for length is the **meter**. The metric system also uses **liter** as a basic unit of volume or capacity and the **gram** as a basic unit of mass. The related units are made by adding a prefix to the basic unit. The prefixes and their meanings are:

MILLI- = 1/1,000	**DECI- = 1/10**	**HECTO- = 100**
CENTI- = 1/100	**DEKA- = 10**	**KILO- = 1,000**

FOR EXAMPLE

millimeter (mm)	= 1/1,000 of a meter	milligram (mg)	= 1/1,000 of a gram
centimeter (cm)	= 1/100 of a meter	centigram (cg)	= 1/100 of a gram
decimeter (dm)	= 1/10 of a meter	decigram (dg)	= 1/10 of a gram
dekameter (dm)	= 10 meters	dekagram (dg)	= 10 grams
hectometer (hm)	= 100 meters	hectogram (hg)	= 100 grams
kilometer (km)	= 1,000 meters	kilogram (kg)	= 1,000 grams

The Metric System *started in France. In 1795 the French Academy of Science announced that the length of a meter was exactly 39.370008 inches. They calculated the length of an imaginary line from the North Pole— passing through Paris—to the equator. Then they divided that distance into 10,000,000 equal parts. One of those parts was a meter.*

QUESTIONS TO PONDER

1. How many meters are there in a kilometer?

2. How many liters of milk would fit in a jug that could hold a hectoliter of liquid?

3. A meter equals how many feet? (*Hint:* Read the sections titled "Did You Know?" to find the answer.)

   a. about 3 feet   b. about 13 feet   c. about 39 feet

4. Which system of measurement do you find easier to use and learn: the metric system or the U.S. customary system? Why?

How to Convert Measurements

Do you want to convert feet to meters or miles to kilometers? You first need to know how many meters are in one foot or how many kilometers are in one mile. The tables below show how to convert units in the U.S. customary system to units in the metric system and how to convert metric units to U.S. customary units.

Converting U.S. Customary Units to Metric Units

If you know the number of	Multiply by	To get the number of
inches	2.5400	centimeters
inches	.0254	meters
feet	30.4800	centimeters
feet	.3048	meters
yards	.9144	meters
miles	1.6093	kilometers
square inches	6.4516	square centimeters
square feet	.0929	square meters
square yards	.8361	square meters
acres	.4047	hectares
cubic inches	16.3871	cubic centimeters
cubic feet	.0283	cubic meters
cubic yards	.7646	cubic meters
quarts (liquid)	.9464	liters
ounces	28.3495	grams
pounds	.4536	kilograms

Converting Metric Units to U.S. Customary Units

If you know the number of	Multiply by	To get the number of
centimeters	.3937	inches
centimeters	.0328	feet
meters	39.3701	inches
meters	3.2808	feet
meters	1.0936	yards
kilometers	.621	miles
square centimeters	.1550	square inches
square meters	10.7639	square feet
square meters	1.1960	square yards
hectares	2.4710	acres
cubic centimeters	.0610	cubic inches
cubic meters	35.3147	cubic feet
cubic meters	1.3080	cubic yards
liters	1.0567	quarts (liquid)
grams	.0353	ounces
kilograms	2.2046	pounds

QUESTIONS TO PONDER

1. Which is longer, a meter or a yard?

2. Which of the following would you measure in liters?

   a. apple   b. apple tree   c. apple juice

3. Look at these two equations: $1 \ square \ yard < 1 \ acre$ $1 \ acre < 1 \ hectare$

   Is a hectare less than or greater than a square yard?

4. Do you think the U.S. should convert to the Metric System? Do you think it's fair to ask your parents and grandparents to learn a different measurement system from the one they've used all their lives?

The Ancient Middle East

4000–3000 B.C.
► The world's first cities are built by the Sumerian peoples in Mesopotamia, now southern Iraq.

► Sumerians develop a kind of writing called cuneiform.

► Egyptians develop a kind of writing called hieroglyphics.

2700 B.C. Egyptians begin building the great pyramids in the desert.

1792 B.C. Some of the first written laws are created in Babylonia. They are called the Code of Hammurabi.

ACHIEVEMENTS OF THE ANCIENT MIDDLE EAST

Early peoples of the Middle East:

① Studied the stars (astronomy).

② Invented the wheel.

③ Created written language from picture drawings (hieroglyphics and cuneiform).

④ Established the 24-hour day.

⑤ Studied medicine and mathematics.

1200 B.C. Hebrew people settle in Canaan in Palestine after escaping from slavery in Egypt. They are led by the prophet Moses. Unlike most early peoples in the Middle East, the Hebrews believed in only one God (monotheism). They believed that God gave Moses the Ten Commandments on Mount Sinai when they fled Egypt.

1000 B.C. King David unites the Hebrews into one strong kingdom. Also, Palestine was invaded by many different peoples after 1000 B.C., including the Babylonians, the Egyptians, the Persians, and the Romans. It came under Arab Muslim control in the 600s and remained mainly under Muslim control until the 1900s.

336 B.C. Alexander the Great, King of Macedonia, builds an empire from Egypt to India.

63 B.C. Romans conquer Palestine and make it part of their empire.

AROUND 4 B.C. Jesus Christ, the founder of the Christian religion, is born in Bethlehem. He is crucified about A.D. 29.

The pyramids of Egypt, built beginning around 2700 B.C., were tombs of the pharaohs who ruled ancient Egypt. Egyptians believed that the pharaohs would need their bodies in the next life. They developed techniques for embalming and drying out bodies so that they could last for thousands of years. The Egyptian art of embalming peaked around 1600 to 1100 B.C. and came to an end around the A.D. 300s. At that time, many Egyptians were becoming Christians, and preserving bodies after death became less important.

Perhaps the most famous mummy belongs to an Egyptian boy pharaoh named Tutankhamen. King Tut, as he's often called, ruled for less than 10 years, in the late 1300s B.C. He died of unknown causes when he was 16. His tomb, discovered in 1922, was filled with treasures.

QUESTIONS TO PONDER

1. How old was Tutankhamen when he died?

2. What is a word meaning a belief in only one god?

3. The world's first cities were built in what modern-day country?

    a. Sumeria   b. Egypt   c. Iraq

4. Which do you believe is the greatest invention of the people of the Ancient Middle East? Give reasons for your answer.

Greek and Roman Gods

The ancient Greeks worshipped many gods, whom they believed lived on Mount Olympus. The Romans had similar gods, but with different names. Here is a list of some of those gods, with both their Greek and Roman names given.

GREEK NAME	ROMAN NAME	KNOWN AS
Zeus	Jupiter	All-powerful king of the gods. Used a lightning bolt to strike down wrongdoers.
Hera	Juno	Zeus's wife and sister. Angered Zeus by playing favorites with mortals.
Poseidon	Neptune	Zeus's brother and god of the sea. He could unleash storms. Sailors prayed to him for a safe voyage.
Hades	Pluto	Zeus's brother, god of the underworld, where the dead lived as ghostly shadows.
Athena	Minerva	Zeus's daughter, goddess of wisdom. Scholars, soldiers, and craftsmen prayed to her for sharp wits.
Aphrodite	Venus	Goddess of love. She could make people fall in love. Using this skill against other gods made her powerful.
Hephaestus	Vulcan	Son of Zeus and Hera, god of craftsmen and blacksmiths. Ugly and lame, he could work magic with a hammer and anvil.
Apollo	none	Zeus's son and god of the sun, medicine, poetry, and music. Every day, Apollo drove his golden chariot (the Sun) across the sky. He was handsome, coolheaded, and fierce in battle.
Artemis	Diana	Apollo's twin sister, goddess of the moon and the hunt. She punished those who killed animals unnecessarily.

———— QUESTIONS TO PONDER ————

1. What was the name of the Greek god of the sea?

2. Only one of the nine planets in our solar system is not named for a Greek or Roman god or goddess. Can you guess which one?

3. Which of the following terms describes a government that is elected by its citizens?
   a. democracy   b. tyranny   c. monarchy

4. The Greeks and Romans described their gods as having human characteristics. Based on the descriptions above, which god are you most like? Explain your answer.

Asian Religions

Asia is the largest and most-populated continent on Earth. Many of the world's religions began in Asia. Two of the most important were Hinduism and Buddhism.

Hinduism

- Hinduism began in India around 1500 B.C.

- There are currently about 820 million Hindus worldwide.

- A long poem about war called the *Bhagavad Ghita* is one of several Hindu religious writings.

- Here are some Hindu beliefs:

  —there are many gods and many ways of worshipping

  —people die and are reborn many times as other living things

  —there is a universal soul known as Brahman

  —the goal of life is to escape the cycle of birth and death and become part of the Brahman

Buddhism

- Buddhism began in India around 525 B.C. by Gautama Siddhartha (the Buddha).

- There are currently about 360 million Buddhists worldwide.

- The three main collections of Buddhist writing are called the *Tripitaka*, or "Three Baskets."

- Here are some Buddhist beliefs:

  —all of life is impermanent, permanence is an illusion

  —desire is suffering; life is filled with suffering because we desire things

  —by overcoming illusion and desire, one becomes enlightened and achieves a state of perfect peace known as *nirvana,* wherein one realizes the oneness of things

━━━ QUESTIONS TO PONDER ━━━

1. In Hinduism, what is the name given to the universal soul?

2. Who founded Buddhism?

3. Hindus believe that after someone dies, he or she is reborn again as another living thing. This is a belief in _____.

   a. polytheism   b. reincarnation   c. nirvana

4. Do you think it is important to learn about and understand cultures and religions that are different from your own? Give reasons why you feel this way.

Modern Europe

Below are a few of the major events that have taken place in the last four centuries and helped shape the history of Europe.

1600s The Ottoman Turks expand their empire through most of eastern and central Europe.

1618 The Thirty Years' War begins in Europe. The war is fought over religious issues. Much of Europe is destroyed in the conflict, which ends in 1648.

1642 The English civil war begins. King Charles I fights against the forces of the Parliament (legislature). The king's forces are defeated, and he is executed in 1649. But his son, Charles II, eventually returns as king in 1660.

1762 Catherine the Great becomes the Empress of Russia. She allows some religious freedom and extends the Russian Empire.

1789 The French Revolution ended the rule of kings in France and led to democracy there. At first, however, there were wars, much bloodshed, and times when dictators took control. Many people were executed. King Louis XVI and Queen Marie Antoinette were overthrown in the Revolution, and both were executed in 1793.

1799 Napoleon Bonaparte, an army officer, becomes dictator of France. Under his rule, France conquers most of Europe by 1812.

1815 Napoleon's forces are defeated by the British and German armies at Waterloo (in Belgium). Napoleon is exiled to a remote island and dies there in 1821.

1848 Revolutions break out in many countries in Europe. People force their rulers to make more democratic changes.

1914-1918 WORLD WAR I IN EUROPE At the start of World War I in Europe, Germany, Austria-Hungary and the Ottoman Empire opposed England, France, and Russia (the Allies). The United States joined the war in 1917 on the side of the Allies. The Allies won in 1918.

1917 The czar (emperor) is overthrown in the Russian Revolution. The Bolsheviks (Communists) under Vladimir Lenin take control. Huge numbers of people are jailed or killed under dictator Joseph Stalin (1929-1953).

THE RISE OF HITLER Adolf Hitler became dictator of Germany in 1933. He joined forces with rulers in Italy and Japan to form the Axis powers. By 1939, the Axis had started World War II. They fought against the Allies—Great Britain, the Soviet Union, and the U.S. By 1945, Hitler and the Axis powers were defeated. During his 12-year reign, Hitler killed millions of Jews (in what is called the Holocaust) and others.

1945 The Cold War begins. It is a long period of tension between the U.S. and the Soviet Union. Both countries build up their armies and make nuclear weapons but do not go to war against each other.

THE 1990s Communist governments in Eastern Europe are replaced by democratic ones. Divided Germany becomes one nation. The Soviet Union breaks up. The European Union (EU) takes steps toward European unity. The North Atlantic Treaty Organization (NATO) bombs Yugoslavia in an effort to protect Albanians driven out of the Kosovo region.

2002 The euro becomes the single currency in 12 European Union nations.

QUESTIONS TO PONDER

1. In which city and country were Napoleon's forces defeated in 1815?

2. Which three countries formed the Axis powers in World War II?

3. Which female European leader achieved expansion during her rule? Which country did she lead?

4. Compare Europe at the beginning of the 20th century to Europe at the end of the 20th century. What would you say is the biggest difference between the two?

Answer Key

Animals

How Long Do Animals Live?
1. the alligator and the humpback whale
2. the chimpanzee
3. 8 times as long
4. Answers will vary.

Endangered Animals
1. A habitat is a place where something lives.
2. the blue whale
3. 6.5 pounds per hour
4. Answers will vary.

Amazing Ants
1. female
2. c. Europe
3. 4100 pounds
4. Answers will vary.

Dangerous Animals
1. It means "100 legs."
2. False. Once they bite their victim, Komodo dragons leave it to die. They come back later to eat the corpse.
3. People have used the poisonous toxin from these frogs on the tips of hunting darts.
4. Answers will vary.

The Arts

Musical Instruments
1. b. woodwind
2. c. percussion
3. a. IN MA ND OL (mandolin)
4. Answers will vary.

Through Artists' Eyes
1. portraits
2. sculpture
3. b. abstract art
4. Answers will vary.

The World of Books
1. dictionary
2. a. fiction
3. Andes Mountains
4. Answers will vary.

Computers

Computer Basics
1. ROM
2. 01000011
   01000001
   01010100
3. 96 bits
4. Possible answers include: bicycle, bicentennial, bilingual, biped, bipolar, bisect, biweekly, etc. These words all have something to do with the number 2.

The Origins of Computers
1. Electronic Numerical Integrator and Computer
2. It was too expensive and complicated for him to build at the time.
3. 1990s
4. Answers will vary.

The Internet
1. Universal Resource Locator
2. b. browser
3. Possible answers include: password, address, phone number, picture, etc.
4. Answers will vary.

Energy

Energy Keeps Us Moving
1. potential energy
2. a force moving an object
3. When a bicycle is still, it has potential energy. When you ride it, it has kinetic energy.
4. Answers will vary.

Energy from the Sun
1. b. gas tanks
2. c. helium
3. plants
4. Answers will vary.

Sources of Energy
1. Iceland

2. fission
3. Possible answers include: resources are running out, air pollution, and dependence upon countries with greater resources
4. Answers will vary.

Producers and Consumers
1. water power
2. b. Iran
3. a. 85%
4. Answers will vary.

Environment

Biomes
1. trees that lose their leaves in the fall and grow new ones in the spring
2. b. coral reefs
3. grasslands
4. Answers will vary.

Threats to the Environment
1. 21%
2. Trees use carbon dioxide and give off oxygen.
3. 67%
4. Answers will vary.

Water, Water Everywhere
1. warm air
2. a. desalinization
3. 90 pounds
4. Answers will vary.

Where Garbage Goes
1. 54%
2. c. burn
3. b. 16 pounds
4. Answers will vary.

Geography

Land and Water
1. Antarctica
2. b. 13
3. a. 10
4. You would begin at Mount Everest and end

at the bottom of the Pacific Ocean.

Mapping the Earth
1. c. the equator
2. oblate spheroid
3. b. North America and South America
4. Answers will vary.

Reading a Map
1. compass rose
2. b. D1
3. c. 13,899
4. Answers will vary.

Volcanoes
1. crater
2. 89%
3. a. Mount Vesuvius
4. Answers will vary.

Earthquakes
1. Richter scale
2. San Francisco
3. b. some minor damage
4. Answers will vary.

Health

We Are What We Eat
1. nutrients
2. Name 2 of the following 3: It keeps your body warm, it give the muscles energy, and it helps keep the skin soft and healthy.
3. 50 calories
4. Answers will vary.

The Importance of Exercise
1. b. oxygen
2. 180 calories
3. a. 75%
4. Answers will vary.

Your Body
1. the digestive system
2. dead skin cells
3. c. climbing a ladder
4. Answers will vary.

Inventions

Healthy Inventions
1. penicillin

Answer Key *(cont.)*

2. Jonas E. Salk
3. An injection that helps protect a person from a disease.
4. Answers will vary.

Communication Inventions
1. Adjust answer according to current year. (In 2003, the answer will be 1898 years.)
2. Sweden
3. Graham
4. Answers will vary.

Making Life Easier
1. 1891
2. 1907
3. c. Mary Anderson
4. Answers will vary.

Entertaining Inventions
1. 1972
2. Vladimir Zworykin, Philo T. Farnsworth, and John Baird
3. 10 years
4. Answers will vary.

Languages

Top 10 Languages
1. b. Hindi
2. Arabic and Bengali
3. bonjour!
4. Answers will vary.

Idioms
1. c. a flash in the pan
2. dogs and wolves
3. to give the responsibility to someone else
4. Answers will vary.

Fun with Words
1. c. level
2. Answers will vary.
3. Tiger Woods
4. Answers will vary.

Word History
1. rugby
2. England

3. leotard and cardigan
4. Answers will vary.

Money

History of Money
1. c. trade
2. b. beans
3. Gold was heavy, difficult, and dangerous to carry.
4. Answers will vary according to country. For U.S.: penny—Abraham Lincoln; nickel—Thomas Jefferson; dime—Franklin D. Roosevelt; quarter—George Washington; 50-cent piece—John F. Kennedy

The Euro
1. a. Sweden
2. numismatics
3. 80%
4. Answers will vary.

What Do You Want To Be?
1. b. professor
2. People are living longer, and so there are more people to be cared for.
3. computer technician
4. Answers will vary.

Making a Budget
1. balanced
2. in deficit
3. Answers will vary.
4. Answers will vary.

Nations

Afghanistan
1. the Taliban
2. five
3. a. baseball
4. Answers will vary.

Canada
1. an Inuit
2. speaking two languages
3. $10
4. Answers will vary.

The United Nations

1. Kofi Annan
2. New York City, New York, U.S.A.
3. 1954, 1965, 1969, 1988, 2001
4. Answers will vary.

The United Nations (cont.)
1. Netherlands
2. 15 nations
3. c. famine
4. Answers will vary.

Numbers

Finding the Area
1. circumference
2. c. 36 sq. cm
3. 3 colors
4. Answers will vary.

Numerals in Ancient Civilization
1. H
2. Answers will vary.
3. a. CDLXXVI
4. Answers will vary.

Planes and Solids
1. a. hexagon
2. c. irregular octagon
3. 100%
4. Answers will vary.

Number Prefixes
1. 5 children
2. 100
3. $24 ($2 per month for 12 months)
4. Answers will vary.

Science

Everyday Science
1. c. white
2. chlorophyll
3. c. rainbow
4. Answers will vary.

DNA
1. genes
2. 10,000 to 20,000
3. They have the exact same DNA.
4. Answers will vary.

The Elements
1. Nitrogen
2. c. quarks
3. b. pie chart
4. Answers will vary.

Some Famous Scientists
1 Einstein
2. Gottfried von Leibniz
3. a. Lovelace & Berners-Lee
4. Answers will vary.

Signs & Symbols

Braille
1. France, Europe
2. red
3. brown
4. Answers will vary.

Sign Language
1. Laurent Clerc
2. b. done by hands
3. wolf
4. Answers will vary.

Road Signs
1. b.
2. c.
3. Answers will vary.
4. Answers will vary.

Code Talkers
1. World War II
2. turtle
3. Answers will vary.
4. Answers will vary.

Space

Our Solar System
1. a. an orbit
2. c. Mars and Jupiter
3. Pluto
4. Neptune (Earth, Jupiter, Mars, Mercury, Neptune, Pluto, Saturn, Uranus, Venus)

The Planets
1. Galileo
2. Venus
3. Jupiter, Saturn, Neptune, Uranus, Earth, Mars, Pluto, Mercury, Venus
4. Answers will vary.

Answer Key (cont.)

Our Moon

1. 38
2. Neil Armstrong, 1969
3. Answer include satellites for weather, communications, navigation, research, etc.
4. Answers will vary.

Space Words

1. Milky Way
2. solar
3. b. satellite
4. Answers will vary. (Subtract student's birth year from 2061.)

Sports

Batter Up!

1. Sammy Sosa
2. separated
3. b. 15
4. Many baseball players were in the military, fighting in World War II.

Football Fantastic Finishes

1. National Football League
2. Joe Montana
3. c. 79
4. Answers will vary.

The World's Sport

1. soccer's international governing body
2. 7 zeroes (240,000,000)
3. a. 6 billion
4. Answers will vary.

Lord Stanley's Cup

1. It's the only trophy that each player on the winning team gets to take home.
2. 54 years
3. 108 years old
4. Answers will vary.

Transportation

Same Distance, Different Times

1. 4 days

2. It means "across a continent."
3. c. 86 days
4. Answers will vary.

The Automobile

1. Ford (or Henry Ford)
2. Zero Emission Vehicles; fuel efficiency
3. Car makers needed less skill and training, which allowed for more affordable labor.
4. Answers will vary.

A Short History of Transportation

1. c. China
2. Sacramento
3. a. Europe
4. Answers will vary.

Travel

World Cities

1. Amsterdam
2. Paris
3. Catacombs are underground passages that contain graves.
4. Answers will vary.

Time Zones

1. Greenwich, England
2. 1 A.M.
3. 8 hours
4. Yes. If, on the day after your birth date, you travel east across the International Date Line, the date becomes one day earlier: your birth date again!

Amusement Parks

1. 1955
2. the Great Depression
3. Sea World
4. Answers will vary.

Roller Coasters

1. Pennsylvania
2. 60%
3. Steel Dragon 2000, Mie, Japan
4. Answers will vary.

United States

The U.S. Constitution

1. c. Preamble
2. a. peace
3. 38 states or more
4. Answers will vary.

U.S. Supreme Court

1. 9 justices
2. The law is struck down.
3. unity
4. Answers will vary.

Famous African Americans

1. Condoleezza Rice
2. c. 1962
3. The Underground Railroad was a network of homes and churches that housed slaves who were escaping to freedom.
4. Answers will vary.

National Parks

1. El Capitan
2. Everglades
3. 1) Yellowstone National Park, 2) Sequoia and Kings Canyon National Park, 3) Yosemite National Park
4. Answers will vary.

Weather

Measuring Temperature

1. 134°F (57°C)
2. –40°F/–40°C
3. 50°F
4. Answers will vary.

Wet and Windy Weather

1. b. up to 250 mph
2. precipitation
3. Answers will vary.
4. Answers will vary.

Clouds

1. cirrus clouds
2. the science of
3. threatening, menacing, evil, scary
4. Answers will vary.

Lightning

1. thunder
2. c. 50,000°F
3. two
4. Answers will vary.

Weights & Measures

The U.S. Customary System

1. 288 square inches
2. 12 teaspoons
3. c. 5,280 feet
4. Answers will vary.

The Metric System

1. 1,000 meters
2. 100 liters
3. a. about three feet
4. Answers will vary.

How to Convert Measurements

1. meter
2. c. apple juice
3. greater than
4. Answers will vary.

World History

The Ancient Middle East

1. 16 years old
2. monotheism
3. c. Iraq
4. Answers will vary.

Greek and Roman Gods

1. Poseidon
2. Earth
3. a. democracy
4. Answers will vary.

Asian Religions

1. Brahman
2. Gautama Siddhartha (the Buddha)
3. b. reincarnation
4. Answers will vary.

Modern Europe

1. Waterloo, Belgium
2. Germany, Italy, and Japan
3. Catherine the Great; Russia
4. Answers will vary.